Four score and seven years ago our fathers brought forth upon this continent, a new nation, conceived in Liberty, and dedicated to the proposition that all men are created equal.

Now we are engaged in a great civil war, testing whether that nation, or any nation so conceived, and so dedicated, can long endure. We are met on a great battle-field of that war. We have come to dedicate a portion of that field, as a final resting place for those who here gave their lives, that that nation might live. It is altogether fitting and proper that we should do this.

But, in a larger sense, we can not dedicate— we can not consecrate— we can not hallow— this ground. The brave men, living and dead, who poor power to add or detract. The world will little note, nor long remember, what we say here, but it can never forget what they did here. It is for us, the living, rather, to be dedicated here to the unfinished work which they who fought here have, thus far, so nobly advanced. It is rather for us to be here dedicated to the great task remaining before us—

that from these honored dead we take increased devotion to that cause for which they here gave the last full measure of devotion— that we here highly resolve that these dead shall not have died in vain— that this nation, under God, shall have a new birth of freedom— and that government of the people, by the people, for the people, shall not perish from the earth.

LINCOLN AND THE GETTYSBURG ADDRESS

Commemorative Papers

University of Illinois Press, Urbana, 1964

Lincoln and the Gettysburg Address

Commemorative Papers

John Dos Passos

Arthur Lehman Goodhart

Reinhold Niebuhr

Robert Lowell

Paul H. Douglas

David C. Mearns

Edited by Allan Nevins

Four score and seven years ago our fathers brought forth upon this continent, a new nation, conceived in Liberty, and dedicated to the proposition that all men are created equal.

Now we are engaged in a great civil war, testing whether that nation, or any nation so conceived, and so dedicated, can long endure. We are met on a great battle-field of that war. We have come to dedicate a portion of that field, as a final resting place for those who here gave their lives, that that nation might live. It is altogether fitting and proper that we should do this.

But, in a larger sense, we can not dedicate — we can not consecrate — we can not hallow — this ground. The brave men, living and dead, who struggled here, have consecrated it, far above our poor power to add or de-tract. The world will little note, nor long remember, what we say here, but it can never forget what they did here. It is for us, the living, rather, to be dedicated here to the unfinished work which they who fought here, have, thus far, so nobly advanced. It is rather for us to be here dedicated to the great task remaining before us — that from these honored dead we take increased devotion to that cause for which they here gave the last full measure of devotion — that we here highly resolve that these dead shall not have died in vain — that this nation, under God, shall have a new birth of freedom — and that, government of the people, by the people, for the people, shall not perish from the earth.

The Everett copy of the Address, in the Illinois State Historical Library.

Preface

The United States Civil War Centennial Commission, created by Congress, has deemed it part of its duty to hold a limited number of ceremonies in commemoration of the chief events of the conflict. It arranged such a ceremony, for example, for the centenary of the Emancipation Proclamation. On a beautiful September day in 1962, at the Lincoln Memorial in Washington, President John F. Kennedy and Ambassador Adlai E. Stevenson among others spoke, Archibald MacLeish read an original poem, and the Marine Band played a special composition by Ulysses Kay. A few weeks after the centenary of the Gettysburg Address the Commission, which had waited in order that the Commonwealth of Pennsylvania might hold its own ceremony on the battlefield, devoted an evening program in the auditorium of the Interior Department Building in Washington to Lincoln's great speech. It was fortunate in obtaining the services of a roster of specially qualified men. They were Mr. Arthur Lehman Goodhart, long Master of University College in Oxford (though an American citizen) and one of the most eminent Anglo-American authorities on the history of law; Mr. Reinhold Niebuhr, who spoke as a theologian; Mr. John Dos Passos, who spoke as a novelist; Mr. Robert Lowell, who contributed both a commentary and an original poem; Mr. David C. Mearns, Chief of the Manuscript Division of the Library of Congress, who presented a scholarly essay on the composition of the address; and the Honorable Paul H. Douglas, Senator from Illinois, who brought his experience as one of our leading public men to an exploration of the significance of the battle and of the long subsequent struggle to give the Negro his rights. The Commission feels honored in laying the fruits of their labors before the public.

Allan Nevins, Chairman

Contents

Introduction

by Allan Nevins

The remarkable expression of national interest in the Civil War, which began with Margaret Mitchell's *Gone with the Wind* and Stark Young's *So Red the Rose,* with Stephen Vincent Benét's poem *John Brown's Body* and Carl Sandburg's four volumes on Lincoln in *The War Years,* mounted to flood tide in the aftermath of the Second World War. A generation inured to battle was at last ready to read about the ordeal endured by its fathers and grandfathers. It was regrettable that so much of the attention to the Civil War was given to military events and heroes as distinguished from the social, economic, and political phases of the long conflict; regrettable that some of the books were poor and some of the commemorations trashily theatrical. Yet the wave of interest did assist the sober study of all American history.

For the Civil War is a subject of tremendous scope as well as compelling power. Its causes alone form a subject of fascinating complexity, involving nearly every strand in the national fabric down to 1861. Walt Whitman declared that the principal taproots of the conflict were the weak folly of the politicians and the weak indifference to principle shown by much of the electorate. Quite so, if we add a statement that the folly and moral lethargy were chiefly exhibited in relation to the foul blot and handicap of slavery. And we can agree with him that the times of Millard Fillmore, Franklin Pierce, and James Buchanan were truly an era of "deformed, mediocre, snivelling, unreliable, false-hearted men." We can also agree that the drift of a great part of the people and the unwillingness to look a generation ahead were most disheartening.

Not all was drift, however. The steady mounting of passion, North and South, is impressive to study. Still more impressive is the awakening of northern determination; the chief events of the 1850's — the Compromise planned by Clay, the Kansas-Nebraska Act of Douglas which destroyed it, the formation of the Republican Party, the Dred Scott Decision, the Lincoln-Douglas debates, the John Brown raid — brought about what a French onlooker termed the uprising of a great people. And the tragic climax of war, the greatest single conflict of the nineteenth century, offers a panorama full of heroism, color, and poignant sacrifice.

The results of the conflict, unfolded from 1861 to the end, were equally complex. It set four million Negroes on the path toward full equality with the white man. It stimulated the march of industrialism and urbanism in the North. Giving the country a single labor system, it established the basis for a more homogeneous nation. It vastly strengthened the central government at the expense of the states and promoted administrative efficiency while achieving full national unity. The tasks of the war required a degree of organization and discipline to which the loose antebellum republic, predominantly rural, had never before been subjected, so that the American people, entering the struggle an amorphous body, nerveless, slack, and addicted to improvisation, came out of it with a new understanding of system, order, and plan. Business, agriculture, the professions, and a variety of socio-economic activities had been geared to the exigent demands of war, and therefore organized as never before. Meanwhile, the American democracy had vindicated in the eyes of Europe its spiritual vigor as well as material power.

In this vindication, leadership was all important. Just as the Revolutionary crisis would have meant far less to America or the world without the half-dozen greatest men it produced — Washington, Franklin, Adams, Jefferson, Hamilton, Madison — so the Civil War would have been deprived of much of its meaning had it not produced Lee and Jefferson Davis in the South, and Lincoln, Seward, Stanton, Chase, and Sumner in the North. Above all others looms its greatest statesman, Lincoln. As practical leader in a terrible convulsion, he had several marked limitations. To say that he was a hesitant organizer and fumbling administrator is to state a clear fact. His training had taught him practically nothing about governmental organization, and the national immaturity was such that he was unable to call to his side many of the men who, by an efficient deployment of northern resources, might have shortened the conflict. In administration he shared a general disability. The country in 1861 had little administrative machinery, and his predecessors in the White House had possessed little administrative talent; some of the most remarkable, like Jefferson and Jackson, almost none. Lincoln had never administered any unit larger than his law office, and his partner Herndon says he did that badly. But if his haphazard, unsystematic ways were sometimes the despair of his associates, in the end they and most of the people of the North recognized his surpassing greatness.

It was a greatness little marred by his shortcomings, for he had qualities far more valuable than a flair for organization or for the efficient dispatch of business. One was his accurate and penetrating insight; his power of clear, logical thought in complicated situations where wisdom and expediency came into conflict and right and wrong seemed blurred. This insight would have availed him little but for another trait, his instinctive courageous adherence to principle. Once his penetration and logic showed him the just course, he held to it unwaveringly. Another of Lincoln's gifts was his remarkable divination of the mind of the best (and most responsive) part of the people. Public sentiment is always a vague, elusive, disputable medley of many currents, many moods; during the war it seemed to shift as incalculably as the hue of a lake under a sky now cloudy, now sunny. But his perception of the precise lengths to which he could go in leading the nation without losing touch with the intelligent majority was extraordinarily keen.

The finest of his attributes, however, was his imaginative sense of the larger meaning of the conflict between union and disunion, between freedom and slavery — his realization that the war was a desperate test on a world stage of the question whether a democracy of continental dimensions and idealistic commitments could triumphantly survive, or must ignobly collapse. He saw the conflict as a struggle of vital import to that growing part of mankind which felt a passionate interest in democracy and freedom — of vital import to the future of the human race. In short, Lincoln was an extraordinary combination of intellect, conscience, and imagination; three qualities often met singly, but seldom together, and still more seldom in such happy balance. Thus the untried Illinois attorney, who entered the presidency amid the doubts of half the North, the hatred of the South, and the sneers of the privileged classes of Europe, emerged from it the most representative figure of his country — "new growth of our new soil, the first American," wrote Lowell — and the greatest leader of democracy in history. The quintessence of much of his thought and emotion is compressed into his Gettysburg Address.

Assuredly, among the events of the war, the Address merits remembrance as much as any battle or any act of statesmanship except the Emancipation Proclamation. It is not difficult to understand why Lincoln consented to set out on November 18, 1863, for the dedication of a national cemetery at Gettysburg. Since the state elections of October and November, he could feel that the tide of popular sentiment was flowing in his favor. On the war front, Grant's timely restoration of communications had guaranteed the safety of Chattanooga, and possession of that vital railroad center, the gateway to Georgia, was an augury of sweeping new advances. Lincoln could well say in his letter to J. C. Conkling, "The signs look better." When David Wills, the citizen of Gettysburg who had proposed the cemetery and who with the support of Governor Andrew G. Curtin had brought it into existence, invited Lincoln to attend, he probably anticipated a refusal. The President's duties were so incessant and onerous that he almost never stirred from the vicinity of Washington. But in this hopeful hour he felt good reasons for accepting. He was influenced by the heartening response to his recent utterances, and by the fact that John Murray Forbes, in praising his Conkling letter, had urged him to expound the great truth that the war was not one of North against South, but of democracy against the foes of democracy.

"Our friends abroad see it!" wrote Forbes. "John Bright and his glorious band of European Republicans see that we are fighting for democracy. . . . The aristocrats and the Despots of the old world see that our quarrel is that of the People against an aristocracy."

The overriding reason for Lincoln's acceptance, however, was that he felt attendance a duty to the brave men, living and dead, who had fought at Gettysburg and on so many other bloody fields of the preceding half-year, from Chancellorsville to Chickamauga. It was a duty to say something that might assuage the grief of the kinsfolk of the slain and uplift the spirit of the nation.

We may be sure that it was in a deeply sober temper that Lincoln left Washington about noon on the 18th. His coach was transferred in Baltimore from the Baltimore & Ohio to the Northern Central line, and toward evening his little special train paused at Hanover Junction to be switched to the Gettysburg tracks. To a knot of onlookers the President, appearing on the platform, made the quaintly jocose remark, an expression of his humility, recorded later in these pages. At dusk he found Gettysburg jammed with thousands of visitors, through whom Wills, Darius N. Couch (leader of Pennsylvania home guard levies in the recent campaign), and Edward Everett drove with him to the Wills house on the public square.

He sat down to dinner that night, still in a sober mood, with Seward, the two other Cabinet officers who had accompanied him, the French Minister, and some high army and naval officers. Everett, who had just toured the field, could speak sadly of the cannon-scarred trees, the raw graves of men buried where they fell, with a bit of wood at head and foot as temporary markers, and the southern corpses in the Devil's Den which had naught but some rocks for covering. This was the first occasion on which Lincoln and Everett had met for conversation. Later, when some Boston friends spoke of the President's lack of social grace, Everett was able to say that Lincoln, as he sat at David Wills's table, was the peer of any person present in manners, appearance, and speech.

The solemnity of an evening in the town that had so lately echoed to the clangor of warring hosts would not have been lost upon Lincoln, and he had a solemn task to complete — his address. The roaming crowds kept up their hubbub; the band of the New York Fifth Artillery serenaded him shortly after nine o'clock, getting, as Mr. Dos Passos here records, a clumsy little impromptu speech in response; and he then retired to his room and worked on the manuscript that he had begun in Washington. It seems likely that he finished or almost finished the address that night and took it next door to show Seward. Perhaps next morning, the 19th, between nine and ten o'clock, he put the final touches on the document. Two facts, as Mr. Mearns shows in his careful essay, are certain: that he gave intense and careful labor, after his wont, to his deliverance, and that it was begun in the White House and completed under the Wills roof — no part of it, contrary to a widely accepted legend, being written on the train.

Early on the afternoon of the 19th, amid a throng of fifteen to twenty thousand people, the procession was formed and set out past the brick shops, the wooden houses, and the leafless trees to the seventeen acres that Wills had bought for the cemetery; a band in front, then a military detachment with sloping bayonets, then the dignitaries (Lincoln looking a bit ungainly on his horse), and finally visitors and townspeople. Although we have some conflicting statements upon the weather, our best evidence is that the day was beautiful, with a bright sun, a crisp breeze, and a crystal atmosphere that brought the blue hills into clear relief. A small platform with chairs, open to the heavens, was provided for the speaker and important guests, but all others had to stand on the bare hilltop, devoid of trees, bushes, or grass. One consequence was that few women, if any, took places in the audience; another was that part of the crowd grew tired and restive during Everett's long address and wandered away. The military contingent, bearing several half-furled flags, lent color to the concourse.

A dirge by the band and a well-phrased prayer by the chaplain of the Senate were followed by Everett's two-hour effort, which he had fairly memorized; a speech that, as Senator Douglas here emphasizes, was worthy of the occasion. It was a polished historical review, using information supplied by Halleck, Meade, Theodore Lyman of the general's headquarters staff, and others, to present an accurate narrative of the campaign and the battle. Fittingly, Everett closed with an argument to demonstrate that as English unity had survived the War of the Roses and the Cromwellian battles, as the terrible hatreds engendered in Germany by the Thirty Years' War had presently died away, and as French unity had arisen purified from the convulsions of the Revolution, so Americans might hope that peace would bring a restoration of unity on a more rocklike foundation. Lincoln listened approvingly, for he wished nothing more earnestly than such a restoration of the old-time union of hearts as Everett foretold.

"There is no bitterness on the part of the masses," declared Everett. "The bonds that unite us as one people, a substantial community of origin, language, belief, and law (the four great ties that hold the societies of men together); common national and political interests; a common history; a common pride in a glorious ancestry . . . these bonds of union are of perennial force and energy, while the causes of alienation are imaginary, fictitious, and transient. The heart of the people North and South is for the Union."

This was the note that Seward had struck the night before, when he made a brief speech to serenaders predicting a happy acceptance by North and South, once

the conflict ended, of both national integrity and emancipation. "Then we shall know that we are not enemies,
that we are friends and brothers, that this Union is
a reality, and we shall mourn together for the evil
wrought by this rebellion." Lincoln might have sounded
the same chord; but he chose to speak not to his country
alone but to aspirants for freedom in all countries, and
not to his own moment in history but to the centuries.
The proposition that all men are created equal was a
truth for the ages, and if America under God achieved
a new birth of freedom, it would stand as an object
lesson to all nations.

Inevitably, Lincoln's immortal speech, delivered to a
crowd numbed with standing, seemed to many an anti-
climax after Everett's stirring peroration, with its quo-
tation from Pericles. Few then grasped the fact that
while Everett's function was to celebrate the glories of
the field and the heroism of the slain, Lincoln's duty was
merely to pronounce a formal dedication of the resting
place. That he had done far more; that he had dedicated
the nation to the defense and invigoration of free institutions wherever the influence of the republic might
extend; that he had written one of the noblest prose
poems of the language — this was at first evident to
only a few men. His "little speech," as he termed it, was
four times interrupted by applause, and was followed by
long-continued handclapping, but he was disappointed
in what he thought its want of impact. Indeed, an able
reporter, John Russell Young of the friendly Philadel-

phia *Press,* wrote later that while Everett's discourse had the perfection of "a bit of Greek sculpture — beautiful but cold as ice," and was impressive as "resonant, clear, splendid rhetoric," Lincoln's speech, delivered in his high tenor voice with not the least attempt at effect, "made no particular impression at the time."

Yet some perceptive men comprehended the august character of Lincoln's utterance, so eloquent in its appeal to the finest aspirations of the nation, and so completely devoid of any note of partisanship, sectionalism, or ignoble emotion. It was unfortunate that newspapers using the Associated Press dispatch had an imperfect version; but others, like the Boston *Daily Advertiser* of November 20, obtained a reasonably correct text. Someone on the staff of the Springfield *Republican,* possibly Samuel Bowles or Josiah Gilbert Holland, hailed it as "a perfect gem." Somebody on the Providence *Journal,* possibly the editor James Burrill Angell, pronounced it beautiful, inspiring, and thrilling. The cultivated George William Curtis asserted in *Harper's Weekly* that the President's utterance, an appeal from the heart to the heart, could not be read without emotion: "It is as simple and felicitous and earnest a word as was ever spoken." Edward Everett generously assured Lincoln that he had said more in two minutes than Everett himself had said in two hours, and Everett was too sincere a man to say this without meaning it.

Throughout the North more and more people comprehended that the President was the nation's greatest single asset. Newspapers were advertising "The President's Hymn," written as a response to his Thanksgiving Proclamation of October 3, which had opened with a poetic reference to the blessings of "fruitful fields and healthful skies," and had closed on a deeply religious note. Henry J. Raymond's *New York Times* had just declared: "In spite of all the hard trials and hard words to which he has been exposed, Abraham Lincoln is today the most popular man in the Republic. All the denunciation and all the arts of the demagogue are perfectly powerless to wean the people from their faith in him." "Wherever I have been this summer," Schuyler Colfax assured the President just after the Gettysburg speech, "I have seen the evidences of a very powerful popular feeling in your favor."

"I don't know," Lincoln remarked philosophically to the radical Senator Lot M. Morrill of Maine, "but that God has created some one man great enough to comprehend the whole of this stupendous crisis and transaction from end to end, and endowed him with sufficient wisdom to manage and direct it. I confess that I do not fully understand and foresee it all." He would not have made this statement had he not tried hard and reverently to puzzle out the meaning of the convulsion for his era and times to come. He put as much of this meaning as his heart and mind could encompass into the Gettysburg Address. Charles Eliot Norton, who had at first doubted Lincoln's qualities, had come around by the summer of 1863 to recognize his power. "He rises with each new effort," Norton wrote in September, "and his letters are successive victories." He demonstrated as no one else had done, added the New Englander, the possibility of uniting a tremendous centralization of power with a direct reliance upon the will of the people. After the Gettysburg Address Norton sent a friend a still warmer tribute: "I conceive his character to be on the whole the greatest net gain from the war." This was an exaggeration, but if we recast the sentence to speak of the effect of his thought and vision upon the American character, we are inclined to say that after a century the statement may well be pronounced true.

Lincoln and
His Almost
Chosen People

by John Dos Passos

The story of that day has been so often repeated that it is as if you had been there yourself. It is as if we personally remembered the neat streets of Gettysburg jingling with horsemen and carriages that Indian summer morning, the ladies in hoopskirts and shawls, the bearded Amish in their flat black hats, the hobbling convalescents in weatherstained blue from the military hospitals, and the gleam of the Marine Band that led the cavalcade of blackcoated dignitaries out the Taneytown road to Cemetery Ridge. Right behind the band President Lincoln's dark gangling frame, topped by a tall silk hat, towers above the dumpy figures of cabinet members and secretaries. For once he rides a horse that suits him, a fine big chestnut. Even his most querulous critics admit that he sits his horse well.

A square wooden platform had been erected at the cemetery. It bustled with governors and congressmen and diplomats, interlarded here and there with a general in uniform. The speakers faced the multitude of raw graves and the shallow valley and the ridges where nearly forty-five thousand men fell dead or wounded in the three-day battle which ended Lee's invasion of the North. Beyond the ridges and the russet woods of late fall smooth blue hills shimmered in the smoky distance.

The opening prayer, which was described as touching and beautiful, was also remembered for its extreme length. Then the band played "Old Hundred," and the stately figure of Edward Everett, ex-Senator, former Secretary of State, four-term governor of Massachusetts, the first American to win a doctorate in a German university, apostle of Hellenic studies, ex-president of Harvard College, Brahmin of the Brahmins, and the fashionable orator of the day, advanced to the podium with a sheaf of papers in his hand.

"Standing beneath this serene sky," he began, in the voice which had been described as equal in melody to that of the prodigious Webster, "overlooking these broad fields now reposing from the labors of the waning year, the mighty Alleghenies towering before us, the graves of our brethren beneath our feet, it is with hesitation that I raise my poor voice to break the eloquent silence of God and Nature."

Mr. Everett's voice broke the silence for something like two hours, according to the reporter from the *New York Times,* who went on to describe the sightseers wandering over the slopes in search of souvenirs, and the great number of carcasses of dead horses which had been left to rot in the fields.

Listeners on the edge of the crowd, too far away to follow the learned Bostonian as he led them, in measured periods, through human history from Pericles' funeral oration to the Union successes of the past summer, may well have been regaling each other with fresh tales of the President's oddities. When he had been called to speak to one throng waiting at a train stop the day before, he had smiled at them wryly from the back platform. "Well, you've seen me," he said, "and according to general experience you have seen less than you expected to see." When a military band came out in the moonlight to serenade him at Judge Wills's house in Gettysburg, he appeared tall and grim at a second story balcony, and told the people thronging the street below he was sure that they would listen to him if he did make a speech but that tonight he had no speech to make. He added that in his position it was important for him not to say foolish things. "Not if you can help it," came a voice from the crowd. "It often happens that the only way to help it is to say nothing at all." The President made his bow and retired. Some people appreciated this kind of humor, but a great many didn't.

It was hard for people to understand that Abraham

Lincoln was not an off-the-cuff speaker. Every sentence he uttered had to be phrased and rephrased, and written out in his careful hand. He had worked long and hard over the scant two pages he was planning to read as his share of the dedicatory remarks.

We were most of us brought up on the story of the notes scribbled on the back of an envelope, but the record seems to show that Lincoln started drafting the Gettysburg Address back in Washington at the Executive Mansion, and finished it at Judge Wills' house before going to bed the night he arrived in Gettysburg.

He was never quite satisfied with it. His invitation to speak was an afterthought on the part of the Cemetery Commission. The press of executive business left him little time to arrange his thoughts for the address. He was preoccupied with the message to Congress he was preparing for early December. In spite of two great victories for the Union cause that had ushered in the summer's campaign, Gettysburg and Vicksburg, it had been a heavy year. Draft riots in New York. Copperhead agitation in the Middle West. At that very moment Bragg's Confederates seemed to have a federal army bottled up in Chattanooga. Grant was on his way to the rescue. After having allowed Lee to make good his retreat across the Potomac, Meade was facing him along the Rapidan. Again Meade had let the wily strategist choose his own ground: Lincoln trembled for the result. As if he hadn't enough public worries, his dearest little Tad had taken sick. He had left Mrs. Lincoln, who had never recovered from their son Willie's death the year before, in a state near hysterics.

Just before starting for the cemetery the President was handed a cheering telegram from Secretary of War Stanton. Grant had things in hand at Chattanooga. Mrs. Lincoln reported the boy was better.

Even so late in his career Lincoln was a nervous speaker. His voice was shrill and his delivery mechanical at the start. Sitting with an air of respectful attention through Edward Everett's oratorical set piece, which a Philadelphia reporter described as like Greek sculpture, "beautiful but cold as ice," Lincoln had time to collect his thoughts. He even made a couple of last-minute changes in the order of words. A hymn, specially composed for the occasion and sung by the Baltimore Glee Club, rose out of the "thundering applause" that greeted Edward Everett's patriotic peroration. During the singing Mr. Lincoln was seen to put on his eyeglasses. He ran his eyes hastily down the two sheets he had brought out of his pocket. His strapping young friend and junior partner Ward Hill Lamon, whom he had appointed a United States marshal and who acted as a private bodyguard, rose to his feet and introduced "The President of the United States."

Accounts differ as to the immediate effect on the audience of the Gettysburg Address. Young John Hay, then one of Lincoln's secretaries, thought the Ancient, as he called him, acquitted himself well. Others found his delivery high pitched and tremulous with taut nerves. A reporter wrote of his "sharp unmusical treble voice." The speech was over so soon that a photographer who had meant to photograph the President delivering it didn't have time to focus his lens. There was applause, but Lincoln felt it perfunctory. "Lamon," he is reported to have whispered to his friend as he stepped back from the edge of the platform, "that speech went sour. It is a flat failure and the people are disappointed."

But the address stuck in people's minds. The more they remembered it, the more they were impressed. Edward Everett wrote Lincoln handsomely next day: "I should be glad, if I could flatter myself that I came as near to the central idea of the occasion in two hours, as you did in two minutes." *Harper's Weekly* in New York found the speech "simple," "felicitous," "earnest." Even among New Englanders who had been so scornful of the rail-splitting attorney from backwoods Illinois the address was spoken of as "one of the wonders of the day."

As the years went by, memorized by every schoolchild, the Gettysburg Address became, along with the Declaration of Independence, one of the grand showpieces of the American heritage.

Why should these few words have rung so true? Why should they have evoked such response from so many different kinds of people? Wasn't it perhaps that Lincoln, by birth and education, was the man of his time best fitted to speak from the main stream of national culture? The great underlying fact which motivated the history of the United States throughout the mid-nineteenth century was the migration westward. As a boy and youth, Lincoln had lived that migration. The inner spirit and the external ethics of the nation were based on the Protestant Bible. The Bible was the mold of Lincoln's intellectual formation.

In that sense Lincoln was the best educated man in the United States. The college-trained gentry along the Eastern seaboard were thrown off by his canny use of the ignorant country-boy pose which he found such an asset politically. They couldn't see that education was a profounder matter than college courses. Literate Americans were still shut up too tight in their provincial backwater of the English literary tradition to appreciate the energy or the depth of the national culture then forming. Based on the Bible and on the traditions of the Scotch-Irish borderers it was part of the main stream of the culture of the English-speaking peoples. As a wielder of words Lincoln was among the forerunners of the new tradition: Lincoln, Walt Whitman, Mark Twain.

Born in Kentucky, where his father and grandfather had moved from Rockingham County, Virginia, as part of the first wave of settlers across the Appalachians, his earliest memory was being told how his grandfather Abraham was killed by an Indian while clearing the forest behind his cabin. Lincoln described his father Thomas as "a wandering labor boy . . . who never did more in the way of writing than bunglingly write his own name." The family legend had it that it was Abraham Lincoln's mother who taught his father that much; certainly she seems to have started young Abraham reading the Bible at an early age.

Thomas Lincoln worked as a carpenter and odd job man. He drifted westward with the tide. Having trouble getting title to the land he had cleared in Kentucky, he moved the family to Indiana where the homesteader had a better chance. Lincoln wrote of himself as a boy as large for his age . . . "and had an axe put in his hands at once; and from that till within his twenty-third year he was almost constantly handling that most useful instrument."

When he was nine his mother died of an epidemic known as "the milk-sick." Thomas Lincoln, who seems to have been luckier with the ladies than with crops or land titles, went back home to Kentucky and picked himself a new wife. Abraham and his sister needed a woman's care.

This was a competent widow with three children, said to have been a childhood sweetheart. Children were an asset to a pioneer family. Many hands made light work. She was tolerably well furnished with this world's goods in the shape of house furnishings and farming equipment, and Abraham Lincoln affectionately remembered her care and kindness. Perhaps she encouraged him to pay attention to his schooling when he could get it, "by littles," he described it.

Abe grew up with a reputation for great strength.

The neighbors thought he was lazy. Most of them agreed with his father that reading a book never cleared an acre of land. A cousin, John Hanks, told Herndon, reminiscing about the days when he and Abe worked together in the field as shambling teenagers: "When Abe and I returned to the house from work he would go to the cupboard, snatch a piece of corn bread, sit down, take a book, cock his legs up as high as his head and read. We grubbed, plowed, mowed and worked together barefooted in the field. Whenever Abe had a chance in the field while at work, or at the house, he would stop and read."

Outside of the famous "school of hard knocks" Lincoln got his early education almost exclusively from the Bible, *Pilgrim's Progress,* and *Aesop's Fables.* The shrewd and salty comments of the Hebrew chroniclers made more of an impression on him than the miracles. He instinctively recognized that the Old Testament encompassed an entire literature; the mythology, the poetry, as well as the traditional history and the religion of the tribes of Israel. Lincoln once remarked that, compared with other books that came into his hand, it was the truthfulness of the characterizations that impressed him. Saul and David were real men. The chronicler did not gloss over their sins and weaknesses. The boy could compare them with men he know.

The border life of the Lincoln and Hanks families wasn't too different from the life of the Israelites. Though there had been some improvement in tools, their technology had not advanced too far from the technology of the days of Abraham the patriarch. Though the machine age was imminent, the first twenty years of Lincoln's life were spent in the age of handicraft.

Pilgrim's Progress and *Aesop's Fables* fitted in with pioneer culture where storytelling was an art. When he came to *Robinson Crusoe,* it fitted in perfectly: that was how young Abe lived most of the time. Added to that were scraps of oratory and quotations from the classics he found in his school readers. From these quotations and from the Biblical teachings, he could assemble a body of standards to judge the world by. Then when he read Parson Weems' *George Washington,* his whole soul kindled with the thought that there were nobler things to do in the world than hoe corn. Ambition started to stir in him to do something grander than splitting rails.

Of course his reading broadened when he moved to New Salem and then later to Springfield. Gibbon gave him a touch of the ironic and Augustan view of history. Volney and Tom Paine disparaged the Biblical miracles that the revivalist sects he was brought up with based their faith on. For a while he fancied himself a freethinker. Eventually the inconsistencies of the freethinkers struck him as forcibly as the inconsistencies of the Biblical mythmakers. He was never a church member and had no interest at all in sectarian dogmas, but in the last analysis he was as profoundly imbued with the religion of the Bible as any man who ever lived.

Lincoln was bound he would push out into the world

for himself the day he turned twenty-one. Before he could leave home he had to help his father's family in one more migration, this time into the black loam country of Illinois. He helped his father build wagons and load them with the plows and the hoes and the bedding brought from Kentucky, and they set off for a new location.

When he described the journey for John L. Scripps, who was getting up a campaign biography in 1860, his words naturally fell into the Old Testament cadences: "March 1, 1830, Abraham having just completed his twenty-first year, his father and family, with the families of the two daughters and sons-in-law of his stepmother, left the old homestead in Indiana and came to Illinois. Their mode of conveyance was wagons drawn by ox-teams, and Abraham drove one of the teams. They reached the county of Macon, and stopped there some time within the same month of March. . . . His father and family settled a new place at the junction of the timberland and the prairie," Lincoln's narrative continued. "Here they built a log cabin, into which they removed, and made sufficient of rails to fence ten acres of ground, fenced and broke the ground, and raised a crop of sown corn upon it the same year."

Compare the cadence with this passage from Chronicles: "And they went to the entrance of Gedor, even unto the east side of the valley to seek pasture for their flocks.

"And they found fat pasture and good, and the land

was wide and quiet and peaceable; for they of Ham had dwelt there of old."

These were probably the last rails Abraham Lincoln ever split in his life. He was on the lookout for better ways of making a living. He once told a friend that his father had "learned him to work but had never taught him to like it." While he still lived at Pigeon Creek, he worked as helper with the ferryman and occasionally brought passengers ashore from the Ohio River steamboats in his own skiff. At nineteen he made his first trip down river to New Orleans as a hired hand on a flatboat.

The family had hardly settled near Decatur before Lincoln began to show interest in public affairs. His signature appeared on a petition to the county commissioners to change the location of the polling place. It was during the political campaign that same fall that he made his maiden speech when the candidates for the legislature came to Decatur. "Pictured out the future of Illinois," noted a listener. He added that one of the candidates said "he was a bright one."

Young Lincoln was an enthusiast for "internal improvements." Steamboats were taking the place of flats and bateaux. The difficulties of a second trip poling a flatboat down the Sangamon and then drifting down the Illinois and the Mississippi to New Orleans brought home the need for quick and cheap transportation to open up the Western country. When he was the Civil War President years later, no one had to explain to Abraham Lincoln the importance of the Mississippi. The knowledge had come with the calluses on his hands as he tugged at the steering oar past the settlement at Walnut Hills that was to become Vicksburg.

This trip was in the interest of a storekeeper named Offutt. On his return Lincoln clerked in Offutt's store and helped him run his mill at New Salem. Clerking in a store gave him leisure to read and to exchange droll tales with the customers. Already he had a local reputation as a storyteller. Lincoln used to figure that his whole schooling barely covered a year, but he could write, read, and spell a great deal better than most of his neighbors. He was in demand to draft public documents. For a while he couldn't decide whether to study law or blacksmithing. The law won out. Old-timers told Herndon that Lincoln was hardly ever seen in those days without a book under his arm. He devoured the newspapers.

When Offutt's business showed signs of going on the rocks, Lincoln decided he had made enough friends around New Salem to take a fling at running for office. The lineups were forming for the presidential contest between Andrew Jackson and Henry Clay. Though Lincoln's family and friends were all Jacksonian Democrats, reading Henry Clay's speeches convinced Lincoln he ought to be a Whig. It was as a Whig he decided to run for the legislature. We tend to forget what a conservative man Lincoln was.

His appeal to the voters was disarming. He discussed the feasibility of constructing a railroad across the state. (This was 1832. Construction was only beginning on the first line of the Baltimore and Ohio. New Salem wasn't such a backwater as people have tried to make out.) Right at the present, reflected young Lincoln, a railroad would cost too much to be financed in Sangamon County. The aspirant legislator presented a detailed scheme for canalizing the Sangamon River. He spoke up in favor of public schools. His arguments in favor of universal education was Jeffersonian: "That every man may receive at least a moderate education and thereby be enabled to read the histories of his own and other countries, by which he may duly appreciate the value of our free institutions"; and he noted furthermore "the satisfaction to be derived from all being able to read the Scriptures." He apologized for his youth and ended on a very characteristic note:

Every man is said to have his peculiar ambition. Whether it be true or not, I can say for one that I have no other so great as that of being truly esteemed by my fellow men, by rendering myself worthy of their esteem. [The phrase still smacks of the copybook: he was just turned twenty-three. That copybook was to become the imperative of his career.] . . . I am young and unknown to many of you. I was born and have ever remained in the most humble walks of life. I have no wealthy or popular relations to recommend me. My case is thrown exclusively upon the independent voters of this county, and if elected they will have conferred a favor upon me, for which I shall be unremitting in my labors to compensate. But if the good people in their wisdom shall see fit to keep me in the background I have been too familiar with disappointments to be very much chagrined.

This was a busy summer. Besides running for the

legislature Lincoln hired out to a certain Captain Bogue who was trying to establish a steamboat service from Beardstown on the Illinois to the fast-growing settlement of Springfield about twenty miles above New Salem on the Sangamon. This was internal improvements put in practice. Lincoln's job was to hew with a long-handled axe, cutting away snags and fallen trees that impeded the passage of the good ship *Talisman*. The *Talisman* never reached Springfield. She stuck on a dam when she had to turn back on account of the falling water. The enterprise was a failure. Steamboating on the Sangamon proved unprofitable. It was probably the experience of this trip that caused Lincoln a few years later to dope out and patent a contraption for easing boats over sandbars.

Back in New Salem with forty dollars in his pocket, and at loose ends, Lincoln enlisted in the militia. The occasion was an expedition to drive Black Hawk and his Sauk warriors back across to the farther side of the Mississippi River. Lincoln was elected captain by his company. Describing his part in that campaign in a sardonic speech he made in Congress many years later, he said he hadn't seen any Indians, but he had shed some blood in his struggles with the mosquitoes. He was mustered out in time to lose his election, but he had the satisfaction of carrying New Salem by a large majority. "The only time," he stated with some solemnity in his autobiography, "that Abraham was ever beaten by a vote of the people."

Well-wishers got him appointed postmaster as a consolation. He picked up a little income as assistant to the county surveyor. Reading the surveyors' manual interested him in geometry. When he was finally elected to the legislature, he took Euclid along to study in slack moments. One of his colleagues lent him law books and eventually took him into his office, when Springfield became the state capital, as a partner. About that time he discovered Shakespeare and memorized scene after scene. Shakespeare's people, like the characters in Chronicles and Kings, were men and women like the people he knew.

According to Herndon, his partner in later years, Lincoln wasn't much of a reader while he was practicing law. Herndon thought he absorbed more information talking to people than reading books.

By the time he became a successful lawyer and married a lady of somewhat upperclass breeding, Lincoln's own education was complete. From the experience of pioneer life and canoeing on the Sangamon and flatboating on the Mississippi and drawing plats for Illinois boom towns and passing the time of day with all comers at the post office, and from absorption in the Bible and from reading Shakespeare's plays and the speeches of Henry Clay, he had already assembled the moral and intellectual tools with which he was going to cope with events and problems for the rest of his life. His outlook was tinged by the crackerbarrel humor of the country store and by a peculiar note of melancholy best expressed by a stanza of his favorite poem, which he found in a newspaper and quoted again and again in all sorts of contexts:

> T'is the wink of an eye, t'is the draught of a breath
> From the blossoms of health to the paleness of death,
> From the gilded saloon to the bier and the shroud.
> Oh, why should the spirit of mortal be proud?

The classics of this particular mid-American mid–nineteenth-century culture formed the mental bank which Lincoln could draw upon whenever political life demanded that he put his notions into words. They had to be words people would understand. They had to be words people would feel. His phrases sank into the minds of his hearers because their education, too, was based on the King James Bible. When Lincoln, in the Gettysburg Address, describes self-government as "government of the people, by the people, for the people" he touched his audience to the quick. The words aroused something more personal than the rubber-stamp response to a political slogan. They aroused unspoken memories of marking the ballots at the polling place, serving on jury duty, petitions to the legislature, political debates in the grand manner, such as the still freshly remembered oratorical contest between Lincoln himself and Stephen A. Douglas which had done so much to polarize Republican opinion during Lincoln's losing campaign for the Senate. Behind the first meanings of the words he used were resonances that struck deep chords of feeling among stored recollections out of Bible reading and hymn-singing in church. To many he seemed a minor prophet come back to life out of the Old Testament.

31

Lincoln never denied that he was a professional politician. He was a professional of self-government. Implicit in many of his speeches was the effort to explain the paradoxical relationship between the leader and the led which was buried deep in the phrase, "government of the people, by the people, for the people." He felt that this balanced interplay was something the people of the United States had that nobody else in the world had. It was easy to feel but hard to pin down in a precise statement.

He had come very close to saying what he meant in an address he delivered before the New Jersey senate in the course of his extended speaking tour on his way to Washington for his first inauguration in the winter of 1861. He had been ingratiating himself with the assembled legislators with reminiscences of what the name Trenton had meant to him:

May I be pardoned if upon this occasion I mention that a way back in my childhood, the earliest days of my being able to read, I got hold of a small book, such a one as few of the younger members have ever seen, Weems's *Life of Washington*. I remember all the accounts there given of the battlefields and struggles for the liberties of the country, and none fixed themselves upon my imagination so deeply as the struggles here at Trenton, New-Jersey. The crossing of the river; the contest with the Hessians; the great hardships endured at that time, all fixed themselves on my memory more than any single revolutionary event; and you all know, for you have all been boys, how these early impressions last longer than any others. I recollect thinking then, boy even though I was, that there must have been something more than common that those men struggled for. I am exceedingly anxious that that thing which they struggled for; that something even more than National Independence; that something that held out a great promise to all the people of the world to all time to come; I am exceedingly anxious that this Union, the Constitution, and the liberties of the people shall be perpetuated in accordance with the original idea for which that struggle was made, and I shall be most happy indeed if I shall be an humble instrument in the hands of the Almighty, and of this, his almost chosen people, for perpetuating the object of that great struggle.

In using the phrase "his almost chosen people" Lincoln was picking his words with care. He was saying that the application of the principles laid down in the Constitution and the Declaration of Independence was a continuing process, not yet completed. This was the theme he resumed in those great phrases in the Gettysburg Address that toll like a bell: "It is for us, the living, rather, to be dedicated here to the unfinished work . . . that these dead shall not have died in vain — that this nation, under God, shall have a new birth. . . ."

A hundred years later what do the words of the careworn national prophet who spoke at Gettysburg mean to us? Have our basic preconceptions changed so completely that we have lost the frame of reference that gave them meaning?

There are two ways of answering this question.

An uncommitted observer from an alien culture (say an Arab journalist) might well search in vain, under the opulence, the crime, the daily exploitation of everything that is shoddiest in human nature which forms so much of the surface of our national life, for any of the deep-seated responses that Lincoln relied on to give meaning to his phrases.

Lincoln was no sectarian, but his outlook was profoundly Christian. Our uncommitted observer might well discover that the bases of Christian conviction were so eroded in the United States that there was little left but the compulsive do-goodism of social service. He might find that the only people who understood what the word liberty meant were refugees from the communist countries where liberty had ceased to exist. He would find the Bible, which was the fountainhead both of individual Protestant Christianity and of the literary tradition of the English-speaking peoples, not only neglected at home, but chased out of the schools. He might suspect that if the atheists carried their victory to its logical extreme, the Good Book might soon be removed from public libraries. He would find that many Americans had so lost faith in the concept of nationality they didn't care whether the United States was chosen or not. He might find it hard to see how Lincoln's words could meet with anything but a perfunctory or ritual response if they were spoken for the first time today.

This uncommitted observer might well discover, against the background of a type of widespread material well-being which the human race has never had to cope with in its previous history, that the concept which for Lincoln was embodied in the expression "the people," had been so disfigured by the manipulations of mass communication as to be unrecognizable. He might even suspect that the technological advances which so changed the shape of society as to raise hob with the ethical norms of the population were in danger of bogging down through a failure of the inventing and improvising imagination. Having read "Mene, Mene, Tekel, Upharsin" off the walls of the banquet hall, our uncommitted observer might well hasten to shake the dust of these states from his shoes. Babylon, too, was prosperous in its day.

But we are not uncommitted. "This nation under God" is our country. "His almost chosen people" is our people. As Americans we are irrevocably committed to that "something more than common" that Washington's Continentals fought for when they surprised the Hessians at Trenton. "That something that held out a great promise to all the people of the world to all time to come" is the cement which reunited the nation when Lincoln won his war against the Confederacy. It is that something added to the political and religious and literary traditions of the English-speaking peoples which has bound together the congeries of immigrants of various origins through the hundred years since Lincoln's short speech at Gettysburg.

It has been a hundred years of dizzy technological development. It has been a period of social change so drastic as to affect the whole gamut of human behavior.

Lincoln spoke at Trenton of his anxiety "that this Union, the Constitution, and the liberties of the people shall be perpetuated in accordance with the original idea for which that struggle was made." This idea was based on belief in individual liberty and individual responsibility. It depended upon the belief that there was a divine spirit in man which ever strove for the good. The truth of this conviction cannot be tested by logic or proved by scientific experiment, but the contrary cannot be proved either. Inevitably the moment comes when we have to take the leap of faith.

Faith is a big word. Lincoln wouldn't have needed to explain it, but today it has become one of those bugle words that leave an emotional blob in the mind instead of a sharp definition. By faith I mean whatever conviction produced a feeling of participation in a common enterprise. A civilization is a common enterprise. When faith is lost, civilizations coast along on their momentum for a while, but soon they start to rot and disintegrate. Much more than on material well-being or on technological successes their survival depends on an inner imperative which causes men to reach for what is good for them instead of what is bad for them. Self-governing institutions particularly depend on individual responsibility for the choice between what is right and what is wrong.

If Americans cease to be dedicated to "that something more than common" that Lincoln spoke of, the republic he gave his life for has no more reason for being. The continuing process that faces the generations alive today is the adjustment of the methods of self-government and of the aspirations of individual men for a full life to the changing shape of mass-production society. There is nothing easy about such an assignment. The alternative is the soggy despotism that pervades two-thirds of the globe. Even partial success will call for the rebirth of some sort of central faith as strong as Lincoln's was. Only then may we continue to entertain the hope that this "government of the people, by the people, for the people, shall not perish from the earth."

Lincoln and the Law

by Arthur Lehman Goodhart

In their valuable book *America: The Story of a Free People*[1] Professors Allan Nevins and Henry S. Commager wrote: "There were two basic ideas in the Colonial period. One was the idea of democracy in the sense that all men are entitled to a rough equality of opportunity. . . . The other basic idea was the sense that a special destiny awaited the American people and that they had before them a career such as no other nation was likely to achieve."[2]

[1] Oxford, 1942, p. 50.
[2] The words "democracy" and "liberty" have had various connotations during different times in American history. A useful statement on this point can be found in Professor H. C. Hockett's *The*

Both of these ideas played a major role in Abraham Lincoln's thinking. Thus in the brief, but important, address which he gave in Independence Hall in Philadelphia on February 22, 1861, on his way to the inauguration in Washington, he said: "All the political sentiments I entertain have been drawn, so far as I have been able to draw them, from the sentiments which originated in and were given to the world from this Hall. I have never had a feeling, politically, that did not spring from the sentiments embodied in the Declaration of Independence."

Of the sentiments contained in the Declaration the most important from his standpoint was the words "all

Constitutional History of the United States 1826-1876, Macmillan, 1939, vol. II, chap. V, p. 74:

"The class which framed the Constitution as a more or less conscious expression of its ideals cherished the concept of an ordered liberty. . . .

"Its members gloried in the principles of the Revolution, by which they meant particularly the freedom from oppressive restraint by government, and the guarantees of the liberties of individuals as set down in the bills of rights, such as freedom of worship, freedom of speech, and jury trial. The right to participate in government was not one of these liberties, although the 'equality' of men entitled all to the benefits of government. The right to direct one's own economic life, an unwritten corollary of the 'new freedom' was especially prized. . . . America was the synonym of Opportunity."

Lincoln himself never attempted to give a precise meaning to the word "democracy." In his speech at Peoria (1858) he said: ". . . no man is good enough to govern another man without that other's consent. I say this is the leading principle, the sheet-anchor of American republicanism." He also said: "As I would not be a slave, so I would not be a master. This expresses my idea of democracy." (Cf. Herbert Agar, *Abraham Lincoln,* Macmillan, 1952, p. 94.)

men are created equal." It is doubtful whether Lincoln ever analyzed in any detail the word "equal," which from the time of Plato to the present day has given so much difficulty to political philosophers. To some this is a statement of fact based on the view that all men, whatever their race or condition, have substantially the same physical and mental attributes and are controlled by the same feelings and emotions, while for others it is the expression of an ideal. On this question Lincoln remained noncommital, because to debate it would have detracted attention from the essential point which he as a lawyer was attempting in almost every speech to drive home. This was that a difference of race could not turn a sentient human being into nothing more than an object of property. A system of law which purported to deny all rights to persons of the Negro race was therefore in conflict with the law of nature which "no human laws should be suffered to contradict." The word "equal" must, at the very least, mean that all men, as human beings, were entitled to "certain unalienable rights among which are life, liberty and the pursuit of happiness."

Lincoln summed this up in his address criticizing the Dred Scott decision[3] at Springfield, Illinois, on June 26, 1857, when he said that the authors of the Declaration of Independence "intended to include all men but they did not intend to declare all men equal in all respects." Because he thought that it was wrong that a Negro

[3] *Dred Scott* v. *Sandford,* 19 How. (U.S.) 393; 15 L. ed. 691.

woman should be a slave, it did not follow that he was advocating racial intermarriage. He concluded that "in her natural right to eat the bread she earns with her own hands without asking leave of anyone else, she is my equal and the equal of all others."

The question whether such an interpretation could be ascribed to the authors of the Declaration was passionately debated before the Civil War, because if they had intended to hold that Negroes should be excluded from all natural rights then the Declaration could not be cited in support of emancipation. On the one hand, it was argued that this was what they had done because they were obviously aware of the institution of slavery, and a decade later the Constitution, which embodied their ideas specifically referred to slavery, especially the third paragraph of Section 2 of Article IV, which provided that fugitive slaves should be delivered up on the claim of their owners.

To this Lincoln answered[4] that the Declaration was stating a universally valid principle in the hope that "enforcement of it might follow as fast as the circumstances should permit." In support of this he quoted the words of Thomas Jefferson, "It is still in our power to direct the process of emancipation and deportation peaceably, and in such slow degrees as that the evil will wear off insensibly. . . . If, on the contrary, it is left to force itself on, human nature must shudder at the prospect held up." Lincoln therefore held that the Declaration

[4] In his Cooper Union Institute Address, 1860.

furnished the strongest support for the view that the extension of slavery would be contrary to the law of nature and in conflict with the basic principles on which a civilized state ought to be based. That debate is, however, only of historical interest today, because the problem of liberty was answered for all time with the end of the Civil War.

But today we are faced with new problems that Lincoln did not have to consider. What are the other unalienable rights to which men are entitled insofar as the state is able to secure these for them? Take the example of education, which is of outstanding interest not only in the United States but throughout the world today. In England during the present century there has been a great revolution in thought on this subject, establishing the principle that all young people are entitled to an equal opportunity to obtain an education, depending on their capacity to benefit from it. That principle has now been accepted by all the political parties.

Or take another problem, closely related to education. Are all men entitled to an equal opportunity to obtain work? Can men be equal, in the sense of the Declaration of Independence, if arbitrary barriers based on race or religion prevent some of them from securing a livelihood? It is not possible to find in Lincoln's own words a solution for these problems because they, of course, were never raised at that time, but I believe that the answer is implicit in his insistence on the unity of all mankind in a common interest in a better and more complete life. In his Philadelphia address he said that the Declaration of Independence had given "liberty not alone to the people of this country, but hope to all the world, for all future time. It was that which gave promise that in due time the weights would be lifted from the shoulders of all men, and that all should have an equal chance." There have been thousands of definitions of the word "democracy," both long and short and in every language of the world, but it is difficult to think of any that is truer or more eloquent than the one found in the three words *an equal chance*.

It was that promise which Lincoln insisted that the American people must keep because if they failed then freedom would "perish from the earth." This was the American destiny; this was the American contribution to the future of the world. The truth of this was recognized across the Atlantic. John Bright, the most eloquent of the British political leaders,[5] reaffirmed in 1863 that the working people in the cotton factories in Manchester were prepared to go hungry so that freedom could be established. Lincoln was urged to stress this in the address he was to deliver at Gettysburg in a few weeks.[6]

[5] It is interesting to find that both Bright and Lincoln had the same sensitivity in the choice of the most effective words. In 1855 Bright, in a speech in the House of Commons denouncing the conduct of the Crimean War, said: "The angel of death has been abroad throughout the land. You may almost hear the beating of his wings." In the original draft of the speech the word was "flapping."

[6] Carl Sandburg has dealt with this at some length in his *Abraham Lincoln: The War Years*, Harcourt, Brace and Co., 1940, p. 458.

Mr. John Murray Forbes sent him this message: "John Bright and his glorious band of English republicans see that we are fighting for democracy: or (to get rid of the technical name) for liberal institutions. The democrats and the liberals of the Old World are as much and as heartily with us as any supporters we have on this side. Our enemies, too, see it in the same light." The young John Lothrop Motley[7] wrote from London to his mother during a black period of the war: "The real secret of the exultation . . . in the *Times* . . . over our troubles and disasters, is their hatred, not to America so much as to democracy in England." It was the destiny of the United States to answer John Adams' dire prediction:[8] "Remember democracy never lasts long. It soon wastes, exhausts and murders itself. There never was a democracy that did not commit suicide."

But it was not only with democracy and destiny that Lincoln was concerned. There was a third basic idea that was greater and more fundamental than either of these, because without it both of the others would inevitably fail. This was the idea of law, on which all stable government must be based. Without respect and obedience to the law, without a sense of law-abidingness, there must follow either anarchy or tyranny. This was the theme of his first formal address, delivered in 1838 to

[7] He later became the famous American historian. (See J. G. Randall, *Lincoln the President,* Dodd, Mead & Company, 1955, vol. III, chap. XIII.

[8] Quoted in Alan Barker's excellent book *The Civil War in America,* Doubleday & Co., Inc., 1961, p. 4.

the Young Men's Lyceum at Springfield. It was entitled "The Perpetuation of Our Political Institutions." He began by saying that there could be no foreign danger to those institutions because no foreign army would dare to invade our shores. Therefore, "as a nation of free men we must live through all time, or die by suicide." This suicide, he said, was, however, an imminent threat because "there is even now something of ill omen amongst us. I mean the increasing disregard for law which pervades the country. . . ."

He pointed out that outrages committed by mobs formed the everyday news of the time and "pervaded the country from New England to Louisiana." Perhaps the most dangerous happenings were in the State of Mississippi where "negroes suspected of conspiring to raise an insurrection were caught and hanged in all parts of the state; then white men supposed to be leaguered with the negroes; and finally strangers from neighboring states, going thither on business were in many instances subjected to the same fate." The answer as Lincoln saw it was simple. "As the patriots of 1776 did to the support of the Declaration of Independence, so to the support of the Constitution and laws let every American pledge his life, his property and his sacred honor. . . ."

At first it may seem strange that a young man brought up in a state that had been a pioneer country only a few years before should have placed so much emphasis on the law, because we tend to think of the pioneers as men who were "trigger-happy." This was, of course, true in part, but only in part because they had already created a system of government that had introduced peace and order. It was based on the heritage of law that had first been brought to the English colonies on the eastern seaboard and had now been carried across the Appalachians to the Middle West. For them it was vivid and dramatic law because as jurymen they themselves played a leading part in it. Their representative was the sheriff whose duty it was to see that order was maintained as the sheriff had done in England for nearly six hundred years.[9]

There was also the judge who rode circuit to bring law to the people, and who was welcomed by the sheriff. Some of the most ancient traditions still remained, although slightly altered; thus the sheriff in Union County would call out as the judge entered: "Oh, yes! Oh, yes! Oh, yes! The honorable judge is now opened."[10] The first log courthouses had been replaced by frame buildings and even by those built of brick, some of which are still standing. The juries were conscious of the authority of the law itself, and that the judge was its representative. Mr. Hill[11] tells of a case in which the jurors were unable

[9] Sir William Blackstone, *Commentaries on the Laws of England,* vol. I, book 1, chap. 9, pp. 339, 343, said: "The Sheriff is an officer of very great antiquity in this Kingdom, his name being derived from two Saxon words. . . . Sheriffs were formerly chosen by the inhabitants of the several counties. . . . As the keeper of the King's peace, both by common law and special commission, he is the first man in the county . . . during his office."

[10] Frederick Trevor Hill, *Lincoln the Lawyer,* The Century Co., 1912, p. 62.

[11] *Ibid.,* p. 68.

to agree. Finally the foreman asked for additional in-
structions. He said: "Judge, this 'ere is the difficulty.
The jury want to know if that thar what you told us was
really the law, or on'y jist your notion." It was to the law
and not to the person that they owed respect.

This recognition by the people that they themselves
were responsible for the law and that it was an essential
part of their lives was an outstandingly important factor
in American history. It was here that they differed most
from the countries founded in Central and South America by the Spanish and Portuguese, because in the latter
the law was imposed and administered by the central
government. To the American pioneer such an idea was
completely alien. The law was his, and it was for him to
enforce it.

It is not surprising, therefore, that Abraham Lincoln,
with his strong feeling of duty to his neighbors, should
have determined to become a lawyer. It has been suggested that he took up the law as a means of livelihood
while his heart was in politics.[12] I do not think this was
probable. It is far more likely that it was his sense of
service that guided his choice of the legal profession.

It is natural, looking back a century, that we should
concentrate nearly all our attention on the ten years of
Lincoln's political life that began with the repeal of the
Missouri Compromise in 1854, for until then politics for

[12] Cf. John J. Duff, *A. Lincoln, Prairie Lawyer,* Rinehart & Co.,
Inc., 1948, 1960, p. 27.

him had played only a secondary role to the law.[13] The only office of real importance that he had previously held was that of congressman in Washington for a single term from 1847 to 1849. There have been twenty-three presidents in the United States who were lawyers, but Lincoln was the only one who practiced the law with hardly a single break throughout the major part of his life before he became President. (President William H. Taft was also a man whose interests were largely legal, but he had been Governor of the Philippines and Secretary of War before his election.) Unless we remember that Lincoln was a lawyer we cannot fully understand the things that he said or did. He was educated by the law, the essential part of his political doctrine was based on the law, and he acted always in accord with the principles of the law. For him law was more than a profession; it was a faith.

Lincoln's legal education probably began when, as a boy in Boonville, Indiana, he first attended a circuit court and watched the legal process in action. To see justice being done, even though its trappings might not be polished, must have been a lesson in law and government that was probably never forgotten. Until 1834 when he was twenty-five years old, Lincoln held various jobs, none of them connected with the law, but there are records to show that from time to time he helped his

[13] During the five years 1849 to 1854 Lincoln devoted his time exclusively to the practice of the law. He wrote in 1859: "I was losing interest in politics when the repeal of the Missouri Compromise aroused me again." (Duff, *op. cit.,* p. 320.)

neighbors in the drafting of simple legal documents. Through his reading of the Bible and of Shakespeare and of a few other books he seemed to have attained a remarkable skill in the use of words in spite of the fact that any formal education he had received totaled less than a year in his whole life. This practice in drafting illustrates the truth that the best form of education is to put one's own words on paper. When he was elected to the state legislature in 1834, his direct connection with the law began, for he was now concerned with drafting bills and resolutions. When the legislature was not in session and when he was able to spare the time from his work as a surveyor or as postmaster of New Salem, Lincoln read law by himself. At that time there were, of course, no law schools. On March 24, 1836, Lincoln was admitted to the Bar of Illinois and began his legal career.[14]

There has been an interesting controversy relating to the law books that Lincoln read as a student. It has been generally agreed that the first book that he studied was the Revised Statutes of Indiana. This was not as dull or as formidable as it sounds, for in its prefix was printed the Declaration of Independence, the constitutions of the United States and of Indiana, and the Ordinance of 1787 for the Northwest Territory. These must have been

[14] Hill, *op. cit.,* pp. 60, 61. In some of the biographies the date is given as March, 1837, but this error is due to the fact that Lincoln's name did not appear on the roll of attorneys until September 9, 1836, and this was not published in the reports until March, 1837.

of intense interest to Lincoln, but whether he read much of the Indiana code itself is doubtful.

Of far greater importance was the next treatise that he read: Sir William Blackstone's *Commentaries on the Laws of England.* To the layman it must always seem strange that a young man living in a little hamlet overlooking the Sangamon River in Illinois should have been concerned with lectures on the laws of England, but the answer is that the colonists had brought with them the English common law, and this law had been stated in a supremely lucid and accurate manner in this work of genius. It is obvious that this law, when transported across the Atlantic, had to be adapted to the novel conditions of a new country, but it is remarkable how few changes had to be made in it, especially in the general principles which were the foundation of the system.

On the strength of a conversation that Lincoln was said to have had in 1860 with the artist Alban Jasper Conant[15] while his portrait was being painted in Springfield, it has become a popular tradition that in 1832, Lincoln, who was part-owner with a man called Berry of a village store in New Salem, purchased for fifty cents from a traveler, who was migrating to the West, a barrel filled with odds and ends, so as to oblige him. He forgot all about it for some time, but when he was overhauling things, he emptied the barrel and found at the bottom of the rubbish a complete edition of Blackstone's *Commen-*

[15] *My Acquaintance with Abraham Lincoln, Liber Scriptorum,* p. 172; *McClure's Magazine,* March, 1909, p. 514.

taries. Albert A. Woldman, in his book *Lawyer Lincoln,* has described in detail this "event destined to shape his career and change the course of history,"[16] and Carl Sandburg has repeated it with dramatic fervor.[17]

It is interesting, therefore, to find that John J. Duff[18] has advanced strong reasons for doubting this story. In 1860, after Lincoln was nominated for the presidency, William Dean Howells prepared a short biography for use in the campaign, in which it was stated that, "He bought an old copy of Blackstone, one day, at auction, in Springfield, and on his return to New Salem, attacked the work with characteristic energy." Lincoln read Howell's manuscript with care, making minute marginal corrections in it, but he made no revision concerning the purchase at auction.

I believe that the latter view is preferable for the following reasons. In 1831 John Reed of Philadelphia printed in four volumes what is known as the *Pennsylvania Blackstone.* It is probable that this is the edition that Lincoln purchased, but it is unlikely that these four volumes would have found their way into a barrel as they were of considerable value and were readily salable as was shown by the large demand for the next Blackstone edition the following year.[19] But a stronger reason for

[16] Houghton Mifflin Co., 1936, p. 14.

[17] Carl Sandburg *Abraham Lincoln: The Prairie Years,* Harcourt, Brace and Co., 1926, p. 163.

[18] *Op. cit.,* pp. 15, 16.

[19] The first edition of the *Commentaries* was printed at the Clarendon Press, Oxford, in four volumes 1765 to 1769. The ninth

disbelieving the barrel story is that it is such a good one. It is most unlikely that Lincoln, who enjoyed telling stories and did not hesitate to repeat them, would not have recognized its dramatic quality, yet none of his legal friends, such as Judge David Davis or William Herndon, seems to have heard him tell it. If a chance event had altered his whole life, would he not have told people about it?

The important thing, however, is that Lincoln did read Blackstone, because from him he learned that the common law is not a collection of arbitrary rules, but is an attempt to express the ideas of fairness and justice that had been developed from the people themselves during many centuries. He learned that government must be subject to the law if it is not to degenerate into despotism and that "the free constitution of Britain" was founded on the English common law, in contrast to "the despotic monarchy of Rome and Byzantium."[20] Here, also, he would find that "the principal view of human laws is, or ought always to be, to explain, protect, and enforce such rights as are absolute. . . ." These absolute

edition published in 1783 was the last one corrected by Blackstone. The thirteenth edition published in 1800 contained important notes by Edward Christian.

The first American edition, printed by Robert Ball at Philadelphia in 1771-72 had 1,587 subscribers. The *Pennsylvania Blackstone* in four volumes was printed by John Reed in Philadelphia in 1831. In 1832 an anonymous edition in two volumes was printed by W. E. Dean in New York City. It contained a limited number of notes on American cases. Further editions were published in 1836, 1838, 1840, 1841, and 1845.

[20] Vol. I, p. 5.

rights of man "are usually summed up in one general appellation, and denominated the natural liberty of mankind."[21]

Most important of all was Blackstone's statement concerning English liberty. "Liberty by the English law depends not upon the complexion; and what was said even in the time of Queen Elizabeth, is now substantially true, that the air of England is too pure for a slave to breathe it."[22]

It is probable that the pages of Blackstone inspired in Lincoln a sense of the importance and drama of history, for almost every rule stated in it is explained and justified in terms of the past, sometimes traced all the way back to the Saxon and the Norman kings. We find a similar historical approach in many of Lincoln's speeches, especially in the famous address at the Cooper Union Institute in New York in 1860, which may be said to have made him President. Senator Stephen Douglas in one of his speeches had said: "Our fathers, when they framed the government under which we live, understood this question [control of slavery in the federal territories] just as well, and even better, than we do now." With this as a text, Lincoln embarked on an analysis of the history to which Douglas had appealed; he must have convinced all those whose minds were not already committed that Douglas had misinterpreted that history.

[21] Vol. I, p. 125.
[22] *Master and Servant,* vol. I, chap. XIV, p. 425.

He was almost Churchillian in his dual concern with the past and the future, realizing that today is only future history. In his Second Annual Message to Congress on December 1, 1862, he said: "Fellow citizens, *we* cannot escape history. We of this Congress and this Administration will be remembered in spite of ourselves. . . . We shall nobly save or meanly lose the last best hope of earth." It may have been this sense of history which enabled Lincoln to face, with unshakable courage and determination, the dark days when the northern armies were suffering defeat and frustration, because the historian, more than most men, places limited emphasis on the immediate present, for he always thinks of events as part of an endless stream.

The three other law books on which Lincoln placed most weight were Chitty on *Pleading*,[23] Simon Greenleaf on *Law of Evidence,* and Joseph Story on *Equity Jurisprudence.* These are probably the most difficult branches of the law, and in them accuracy of language is of major importance. This was true, in particular, of the law of procedure, both civil and criminal, at that time because it still contained many of the technicalities which its practitioners claimed, with some pride, had made it an exact science.[24] Lincoln spoke with respect of a judge of whom he said: "He would hang a man for blowing his nose in the street but he would quash the

[23] The full title was J. Chitty *Treatise on Pleading and Parties to an Action.* Cf. M. L. Houser *Lincoln's Education and Other Essays,* Twayne Publishers.

[24] Cf. Hill, *op. cit.,* chap. III.

indictment if it failed to specify what hand he blew it with." It is not fanciful to suggest that a long training in such a precise use of words must have played an important part in establishing the clarity of Lincoln's style. At a time when the ideal of oratory was found in ornate and resounding phrases, such as were used by Edward Everett[25] in his much admired speech at Gettysburg, Lincoln's austerity was a new departure. It is not surprising that some of those who first heard the Gettysburg Address failed to recognize its supreme artistry. In it there is not a single unnecessary word. Nor is it a coincidence that such words as "proposition" and "dedicate" are those that a lawyer would naturally use. Perhaps it was for this reason that the word "proposition" so offended the finer susceptibilities of Matthew Arnold, who was of a more romantic turn of mind, that he refused to continue reading the Address after meeting this stumbling block in the second line.[26]

The rules of pleading may also have contributed to

[25] It is not fair to the reputation of Edward Everett that the only thing that most people remember about him is that he gave an oration, lasting nearly two hours, before Lincoln delivered the Gettysburg Address. He was a man of firm character, capable of expressing himself in clear and forceful words. When he was president of Harvard from 1846 to 1849 he refused to draw the color line, saying in the case of Beverly Williams, a Negro applicant, that admission to Harvard College depended on examinations. "If this boy passes the examinations, he will be admitted; and if the white students choose to withdraw, all the income of the College will be devoted to his education." (See Sandburg, *Abraham Lincoln: The War Years*, p. 453.)

[26] Herbert J. Edwards and John E. Hawkins in *Lincoln the Writer,* University of Maine Studies, 1962, p. 106.

the brevity of Lincoln's speeches which tended to be brief even by modern standards; thus his Second Inaugural Address must be almost the shortest inaugural on record. The explanation may, perhaps, be found in a letter that he wrote on another occasion to his friend General Linder:[27] "In law it is good policy never to plead what you need not, lest you oblige yourself to prove what you cannot."

Just as there never was an unnecessary phrase in any of his speeches, so there never was a flamboyant one. His enemies accused him of many things, but they never suggested that he was guilty of an exaggeration or of an untruth. Lincoln realized that what you cannot prove had better be left unsaid. He was not afraid of leaving things out because he disliked prolixity, especially if it was irrelevant. Of an opponent he said: "He can compress the most words into the smallest ideas of any man I ever met." He was accused of telling too many humorous stories, and there is some truth in the charge, but they were always in point and as brief as possible. The facts were stated as if he were writing the headnote of a case in the law reports.

It is also of interest to note how effectively he used the

[27] Hill, *op. cit.,* p. 155. A similar story is given by Duff, *op. cit.,* p. 201: "The Squire [the local justice of the peace] recalled Lincoln coming to his office one day, sitting at a table, taking half a sheet of paper and proceeding to write out a declaration. When the Squire remarked on the fact that it was a mighty small piece of paper on which to write a declaration, Lincoln replied 'that he had always found it best to make few statements, for if he made too many the opposite side might make him prove them.' "

repetition of words and phrases to drive home the effect of what he was saying. Thus in the twenty lines of the Gettysburg Address the word "dedicate" is repeated six times, and "lives" and "living" four times. This tends to be the mark of the legal draftsman, for he is taught always to use the same word for the same things. A synonym, which may appeal to those who are particularly concerned with the aesthetic effect that their words may produce, tends to be dangerous in the law, because it may suggest that a subtle difference in meaning is implied by a shift in the words used.

Another legal trait can be found in Lincoln's frequent use of what he himself had said on a previous occasion, or in his borrowing whole sentences from other writers without referring to his sources. The best-known illustration of this is the famous phrase "government of the people, by the people, for the people" in the last line of the Address. This had, almost certainly, been taken from an address delivered by Theodore Parker, an abolitionist preacher, in 1850.[28] He had said: "This [American] idea, demands . . . a democracy, that is a government of all the people, by all the people, for all the people. . . ." Lincoln improved it by leaving out the word "all."[29] Such borrowing is intentionally used by most lawyers because their whole training is directed to reliance on precedents; for them a legal statement has added force

[28] *Speeches, Addresses, and Occasional Discourses,* Boston, 1852.
[29] In his Special Session Message, July 4, 1861, Lincoln spoke of "a government of the people by the same people."

if it can be shown that it is not a novel one. The highest compliment that can be paid to a lawyer is to say that he is a sound thinker; it is less flattering to suggest that he is an original one.

But the most important part of Lincoln's education came from his practice in addressing juries and in arguing cases in the appellate courts, for here he learned how men thought. As a trial lawyer he learned that nothing is more persuasive than a strictly logical argument that a jury can follow and understand. To strengthen his logic he supplemented his legal experience by a study of geometry, carrying a copy of Euclid in his saddlebags as he rode the circuit.[30]

He was never a fluent speaker because, as he himself said, he was a slow thinker; perhaps it would be more correct to say that his passion for accuracy made him hesitate before he spoke. But in the courtroom, when he had prepared his case and knew exactly what he wanted to say, there was no difficulty in finding the appropriate words. They were always simple and direct. When he finally addressed the great jury of his countrymen during the Lincoln-Douglas debates, he followed the same guide rule. As John P. Frank has said in his recent book *Lincoln as a Lawyer*:[31] ". . . he conceived of the debates as a kind of tussle with another lawyer for the purpose of

[30] Hill, *op. cit.*, p. 198.

[31] University of Illinois Press, 1961, p. 125. At p. 111, Frank writes: ". . . his custom of resolving public problems in terms of legal concepts did become a dominant part of his intellectual approach."

persuading a jury of electors." No one can read his speeches without realizing their carefully constructed logical structure. Each sentence and each idea fits into the next one until the inevitable conclusion is reached. In his Freeport speech, which destroyed Senator Douglas' hope of the presidency, he built up his argument until the climax was reached in the second interrogatory which he, thinking as a lawyer, demanded that his opponent should answer: "Can the people of a United States Territory, in any lawful way, against the wish of any citizen of the United States, exclude slavery from its limits prior to the formation of a State Constitution?" Douglas tried to answer this and failed.[32] It was this same logic and unity of structure that gave to the Gettysburg Address its overwhelming power.

It would be pleasant to attribute Lincoln's honesty to his legal training, but his insistence on truthfulness was a trait that had been his from early childhood; the nickname "Honest Abe" that his friends affectionately gave him marked their recognition of his complete reliability. It was natural, therefore, that in his "Notes for a Law Lecture,"[33] which apparently was never delivered, he should have referred to the "vague popular belief that lawyers are necessarily dishonest." His answer was: "Let

[32] Douglas replied that the territories could exclude slavery by adopting local police regulations so hostile to slavery that no slaveowner could enjoy his property within their boundaries. It was this answer which persuaded the southern delegates to reject Douglas at the Democratic Convention in 1860. Senator Judah P. Benjamin denounced his answer.

[33] Written in 1850.

no young man choosing the law for a calling for a moment yield to the popular belief — resolve to be honest at all events; and if in your own judgment you cannot be an honest lawyer, resolve to be honest without being a lawyer."

Lincoln's whole career showed that he believed that a lawyer, more than almost any other man, must be honorable. It is, therefore particularly unfortunate that there is still a popular tradition that in the famous Armstrong murder case Lincoln tricked the judge and the jury.[34] The prisoner was charged with having murdered a man with whom he had quarreled by hitting him with a slingshot. A witness for the prosecution testified that he had seen him strike the blow at about eleven o'clock at night, and that he could see this clearly because the moon was almost full. On cross-examination Lincoln produced a calendar showing that the moon was only at its first quarter, so that it was dark at the time. After the prisoner had been acquitted a rumor developed that Lincoln had substituted an old calendar for the correct one, which would have shown that the witness was telling the truth. It has not been difficult to disprove this story by checking the correct calendar of that year, which shows that the moon was, in fact, at its first quarter, but the story still continues. Some people think that it redounds to Lincoln's credit as showing what a clever lawyer he was, but

[34] Duff, *op. cit.,* pp. 350-359. In 1863 when Armstrong was ill in an Army hospital in Louisville, Kentucky, Lincoln ordered him discharged from the Army on the plea of his mother.

this was the sort of cleverness that he himself would have repudiated with indignation.

It has also been suggested that Lincoln was never more than a small-town lawyer, who had had no experience in the conduct of any important cases. The late Professor Randall in his book *Lincoln, the Liberal Statesman*[35] pointed out how misleading this idea was. "To speak of Lincoln as a country lawyer is to misapply the term. . . . Lincoln's name as a lawyer carried prestige throughout the State. . . . He was an outstanding leader at the bar. . . ."[36] Perhaps the misconception concerning Lincoln's legal career was due less to ill will on the part of his enemies than it was to a sense of the dramatic on the part of those who wished to draw a picture of a back-woodsman suddenly elevated to the White House. Lincoln's modesty and simplicity may have contributed to this, because he never gave the impression of being a successful lawyer. They misled Edwin M. Stanton, a leading lawyer from Pennsylvania, who was brought to Cincinnati in 1855 to represent the defendants as chief counsel in the important reaper patent case, *McCormick v. Manny,* in the federal court. When he found that

[35] Dodd, Mead & Company, 1947.

[36] Hill, *op. cit.,* p. 248, states that in his twenty-three years at the bar in Illinois Lincoln had no less than 172 cases before the highest court of Illinois, a record unsurpassed by any of his contemporaries. He also appeared before United States circuit and district courts with great frequency, and he tried more cases on the Eighth Circuit than any other lawyer. He was counsel for the Illinois Central Railroad, the Rock Island Railroad, and other important corporations.

Lincoln had also been retained, he asked, "Where did that long-armed creature come from, and what does he expect to do in this case?"[37] He refused to let him take any part in the trial. Seven years later Lincoln appointed Stanton as Secretary of War because he was the man best qualified for the post. Of him Lincoln said: "He is a great man, even if he does know it."

The law, however, did more for Lincoln than give him professional distinction. It was the foundation on which all of his political ideas were based. This is not surprising because the immediate point at issue between the North and the South before secession was a legal one: Could the majority of the settlers in a territory exclude slavery? Could the federal government under the Constitution exclude slavery from the territories? It was the decision of Chief Justice Taney and the majority of the Supreme Court in the Dred Scott case in 1857 that brought this quarrel to fever heat because it answered both the questions in the negative. It even suggested that the northern states themselves might be open to slavery. In his debates with Douglas, Lincoln recognized that the decision in the Dred Scott case must be obeyed, but he argued that it could be overruled in some subsequent case. It is of interest that in *Lewis* v. *Lewis*,[38] the only case which he himself had argued in the Supreme Court, that court had,

[37] Hill, *op. cit.*, pp. 257, 258. Duff, *op. cit.*, pp. 323, 324, states that Stanton referred to Lincoln as "that long-armed baboon," and "that giraffe."

[38] (1849) 12 L. ed. 909.

in deciding against him, refused to follow one of its own previous decisions that was in his favor. The force of precedents was of special interest to him as a lawyer, and in his address on the Dred Scott decision at Springfield on June 26, 1857, he explained its effect to the nonlegal audience:

Judicial decisions have two uses — first, to absolutely determine the case decided, and secondly, to indicate to the public how other similar cases will be decided when they arise. . . . We think its decisions on Constitutional questions, when fully settled, should control, not only the particular cases decided, but the general policy of the country, subject to be disturbed only by amendments of the Constitution as provided in that instrument itself. More than this would be revolution. But we think the Dred Scott decision is erroneous. We know the court that made it, has often over-ruled its own decisions, and we shall do what we can to have it over-rule this. We offer no *resistance* to it.

The promise of no resistance did not satisfy the South because it was of only limited value. The Supreme Court had decided the Dred Scott case by a bare majority of five to four, so that if any one of the five should vacate his seat owing to death or resignation, his successor could swing the decision the other way. The election of a Republican President would almost certainly lead to such a result, because the choice of a successor would at some time during the next four years be in his hands.

The election of Lincoln, therefore, led directly to secession. In the four intervening months before the inauguration President Buchanan could not make up his mind concerning the legal effects of secession and what his own legal duties were. Thus Seward, in referring to President Buchanan's Message to Congress in December, 1860, said that it conclusively proved first, that no state had the right to secede unless it wanted to, and second, that it was the President's duty to enforce the law unless somebody opposed him. Lincoln had no such hesitation, as he made clear in his First Inaugural Address. His principles were simple and inflexible. As government was based on law, it followed that the Constitution must be the supreme law of the land. Secession was the denial of that law because no constitution could envisage its own destruction. If it was destroyed then all the hopes of freedom and of justice which the people of the United States and of the world had placed in it would be ended. He concluded that: "Plainly the central idea of secession is the essence of anarchy. . . . The rule of a minority, as a permanent arrangement, is wholly inadmissible; so that, rejecting the majority principle, anarchy or despotism in some form is all that is left." To prevent this he was prepared to fight a war. This was the thesis of the Gettysburg Address.

It was because of his devotion to the Constitution that Lincoln, as a lawyer, took what seemed to many people a hesitant approach to the emancipation of the slaves. "I have no purpose," he said in his First Inaugural, "directly or indirectly, to interfere with the institution of slavery in the States where it exists. I believe I have no lawful right to do so, and I have no inclination to do so."[39] There are many people who do not realize that the Constitution gives only limited powers to the federal government, reserving to the states those matters that are solely of internal concern. There was, therefore, at that time no power that Congress could exercise to abolish slavery in whole or in part.

A new situation arose, however, with secession, because now it could be argued that in certain circumstances, the war power vested in the President included the power to emancipate the slaves who were in the states that had seceded. It was strictly limited to them, because freeing the slaves in the border states, which had remained part of the Union, could not be said to contribute to the successful prosecution of the war. In these circumstances Lincoln hesitated for nearly two years before issuing the Emancipation Proclamation to the disappointment of some of the abolitionists who feared that he was betraying their cause. They remembered that in his First Inaugural Address he had said that the clause in the Constitution providing for the delivering up of fugitive slaves[40] was binding. William Lloyd Garrison at one time referred to Lincoln as "the slave hound of Illinois."

It was especially among the European liberals that his

[39] In an often quoted letter to Horace Greeley of the *New York Tribune* Lincoln wrote: "My paramount object in this struggle is to save the Union, and is not either to save or to destroy slavery. If I could save the Union without freeing any slave, I would do it; and if I could do it by freeing all the slaves, I would do it; and if I could save it by freeing some and leaving others alone, I would also do that."

[40] Article IV, sec. 2 [3].

delay was criticized, for they did not understand the problems to which a federal constitution gave rise. To some of them the Civil War seemed to be justified only if it was being fought to free the slaves. The assumption that secession must be wrong was not self-evident to them. Although the phrase "self-determination" had not been invented at that time, they could not understand why the southern states were not justified in demanding independence. The American colonies had fought for their freedom from England, so why could not some of the former colonies be separated from the others? They did not realize that the Civil War was being fought because the dissolution of the Union would destroy the American destiny. As Lincoln said, "Physically speaking, we cannot separate. A husband and wife may be divorced . . . but the different parts of our country cannot do this." He came from Indiana and Illinois, two states that owed their existence to the national government, so that it was natural that he should feel special devotion to the Constitution and be prepared to sacrifice everything in its defense.[41]

In spite of this devotion Lincoln violated the specific provisions of the Constitution more often than any other

[41] It is understandable that a different point of view should have been held in a state such as Virginia, with its long history antedating the creation of the United States itself.

Lincoln's devotion to the Union may also have been affected by the fact that it was essential for the states in the Middle West that the control of the Mississippi Valley should be maintained as a single whole. The river was the main highway for all traffic so that its freedom must be assured.

President has ever done. He was therefore accused of being a hypocrite, but he had no choice. When the attack on Fort Sumter took place, Congress was not in session, so that all effective action had to be taken by the President alone. His powers were extensive, as Article II, section 1 [1] provides that the executive power shall be vested in a President, and section 2 [1] states that "the President shall be Commander in Chief of the Army and Navy," and "of the Militia of the several States, when called into the actual Service of the United States." The difficulty that faced Lincoln was that Article I gave to Congress all legislative powers, including the power to raise and support an Army and Navy and to call for the militia. Lincoln felt that he could not wait while Congress reconvened and debated, so he acted without its authority.

Of greatest interest was the suspension of the writ of habeas corpus in some of the states in which there was danger of rebellion. The Constitution provides (Art. I, Sec. 9 [2]) that "The Privilege of the Writ of Habeas Corpus shall not be suspended, unless when in Cases of Rebellion or Invasion the public safety may require it." It does not say who shall have the power of suspension, but as the provision is in Article I which begins by stating that all legislative powers shall be vested in Congress, it obviously points to Congress. Moreover, when the provision was made part of the Constitution, some of its framers must have known that Blackstone in speaking of the suspension of the writ in England said:[42] "And yet sometimes, when the state is in real danger, even this may be a necessary measure. But the happiness of our constitution is that it is not left to the executive power to determine when the danger of the state is so great as to render this measure expedient; for it is the Parliament only . . . that, whenever it sees proper, can authorize the Crown, by suspending the *habeas corpus* Act for a short and limited time, to imprison suspected persons without giving any reason for doing so."

In *Ex parte Merryman*[43] the aged Chief Justice Taney, sitting in the federal circuit court, held that the President could not constitutionally suspend the writ, but Lincoln disregarded his opinion, saying that Blackstone did not have to consider a situation in which Parliament was not in a position to act. But even if he himself did not have the strict legal right to suspend the writ, he felt that he was justified in doing so because disloyal men might destroy the country if they could not be imprisoned. In his Message to Congress on July 4, 1861, he said: "Are all the laws *but one* to go unexecuted, and the government itself go to pieces lest that one be violated?" Lincoln did not deny that some of the steps he had taken might be of doubtful constitutional validity, but he justified them on the ground that[44] "as commander-in-chief . . . I suppose I have a right to take any measure which may best subdue the enemy."

[42] Vol. I, page 136.

[43] 17 Federal Cases 144 (No. 9, 487) (C.C. D. Md., 1861).

[44] *The Collected Works of Abraham Lincoln,* Roy P. Basler, ed., Rutgers University Press, 1953, pp. 31-32.

Lincoln also had difficulty with the courts in the four prize cases[45] which came before the Supreme Court in 1863. The validity of the blockade that Lincoln had instituted in 1861 was upheld by five to four, the majority rejecting the "anomalous doctrine . . . that insurgents who have risen in rebellion against their sovereign, expelled her courts, established a revolutionary government, organized armies, and commenced hostilities, are not enemies because they are traitors."

In the field of international law by far the most important case was that of the mail steamer *Trent,* which nearly led to war between Great Britain and the United States. Captain Wilkes of the United States Navy forcibly removed from the *Trent* two emissaries of the Confederacy, Mason and Slidell, who were en route to England and France. The British government demanded their immediate release. The international law on this point was not clear, and public opinion in the North strongly favored a refusal. Fortunately, the Atlantic cable had broken down so that there was time for second thoughts. Lincoln,[46] in spite of a contrary view expressed by two distinguished international lawyers, held that the British had the law on their side, and that this was in accord with what the United States itself had insisted was the law in 1812. If he had been a less able lawyer there would probably have been no United States today.

Perhaps to those who have lived through two world

[45] 67 U.S. (2 Black) 635.
[46] Hill, *op. cit.,* pp. 121, 122.

wars, the most remarkable thing is not that the Constitution was stretched in 1861, but that it was stretched so little. There was no Espionage Act or Sedition Law. Freedom of speech was preserved to the point at which it was difficult to distinguish freedom from treason. Here the *Vallandigham* case[47] can be compared with the *Abrams* case[48] and its litmus-paper sedition. Perhaps the most striking thing, as we look back, was the freedom of the press exercised by some of the newspapers in their vitriolic attacks on the President and on his conduct of the war. Even the Gettysburg Address was held up to ridicule and contempt.

It was Lincoln's hatred of despotic rule and the law-mindedness of the American people which maintained the Constitution in spirit and in fact against the dangers of arbitrary government. This is the lesson that many people have tended to forget or have never learned today. It has become the practice to believe that if a country is given the forms of democratic constitutional government then a major task has been accomplished, but experience

[47] *Ex parte Vallandigham,* 68 U.S. (1 Wall.) 243 (1864). For a statement of the facts in this case, see J. G. Randall, *Constitutional Problems Under Lincoln,* University of Illinois Press, 1951, p. 176.

[48] *Abrams* v. *United States,* 250 U.S. 616 (1919). In his famous dissenting opinion Justice Holmes said: "Even if I am technically wrong and enough can be squeezed from these poor and puny anonymities to turn the color of legal litmus paper . . . the most nominal punishment seems to me all that possibly could be inflicted, unless the defendants are to be made to suffer not for what the indictment alleges but for the creed that they avow. . . ." The defendants had been sentenced to twenty years' imprisonment.

has shown that without an effective system of law, based on the law-mindedness of the people, such a paper constitution is valueless. To Lincoln such words as democracy, equality, and freedom were meaningless unless they were a living truth.

But to Lincoln the most important idea that the law represented was the idea of fairness. Justice carries a pair of scales that are evenly balanced. The basic principle of legal justice was expressed two thousand years ago in the words *audi alteram partem:* You must listen to what the other man has to say. That is the spirit of tolerance of which he was the supreme exemplar. He did not believe that the southerners were wicked or cruel or traitorous; he believed that they were mistaken.[49] When he spoke in the Gettysburg Address of "the great task remaining before us," he was referring not only to victory in the war; he was thinking of a new birth of freedom which recognizes that all men must be given an equal chance. That was the faith of the sad, careworn man who was killed in Ford's Theatre in Washington nearly a hundred years ago. That was the same guiding faith of the gallant and gay young man whom we mourn today. To both of them America meant more than power or wealth or material well-being: it meant that dedication to fairness and tolerance for which they were prepared to lay down their lives.

[49] In his speech at Springfield, closing the senatorial campaign against Stephen A. Douglas, October 30, 1858, Lincoln said: "I have constantly declared, as I really believed, the only difference between them and us, is the difference of circumstances."

The Religion
of Abraham Lincoln

by Reinhold Niebuhr

An analysis of the religion of Abraham Lincoln in the context of the traditional religion of his time and place and of its polemical use on the slavery issue, which corrupted religious life in the days before and during the Civil War, must lead to the conclusion that Lincoln's religious convictions were superior in depth and purity to those, not only of the political leaders of his day, but of the religious leaders of the era.

This judgment may seem extravagant, and the casual reader may suspect that the hagiography which envelopes the heroes of a nation, substituting symbolic myths for sober reality, may have influenced the judgment. It is true, of course, that Lincoln, the savior, and therefore the second father of his nation, is enveloped in historical myth, because nothing but poetic symbol is adequate to express the status of Lincoln as a symbol representing American democracy more accurately than the eighteenth century aristocrat, George Washington, who has first place in the national pantheon as the "father" of his country.

It is nevertheless easy to validate the judgment as sober history, uninfluenced by the usual hagiography of the nations and their heroes. Lincoln's superior religious convictions are partly attested by the fact that, though of deeply religious temperament, he never explicitly joined the religious sects of the frontier. This fact has given occasion for some historians to number Lincoln among the religious sceptics. Lincoln was not a sophisticated modern, but he was a thoughtful and well-read man, and one must suppose that he, therefore, did not share the orthodox beliefs of the frontier, or make common cause with the frontier evangelist, Peter Cartright, incidentally a political opponent of his. Lincoln's religious faith was primarily informed by a sense of providence, an inclination which he shared with most of the world's statesmen.

In his eloquent Second Inaugural Lincoln expressed this sense of providence in these words, "The Almighty has His own purposes. 'Woe unto the world because of offences! for it must needs be that offences come; but woe to that man by whom the offence cometh!' If we shall suppose that American Slavery is one of those offences, which, in the providence of God, must needs come, but which, having continued through His appointed time, He now wills to remove, and that He gives to both North and South, this terrible war, as the woe due to those by whom offence came, shall we discern therein any departure from those divine attributes, which the believers in a Living God always ascribe to Him?" It will be noted that the pious and the sceptical note in Lincoln's faith are both expressed in these words. He speaks of the "divine attributes which the believers in a Living God always ascribe to Him." He does not explicitly number himself among the believers. As he goes on to spell out the workings of providence, one may easily note why there was in him, as in all men, except the most conventional believers, both faith and scepticism in the concept of providence. For the drama of history is shot through with moral meaning; but the meaning is never exact. Sin and punishment, virtue and reward are never precisely proportioned.

Lincoln spells out the dilemma of faith, as he expounds the idea of providence on the issue of slavery; for in the words of Scripture, his conception involves that the "sins of the fathers" are visited on the children of another generation. Lincoln continues "Fondly do we hope — fervently do we pray — that this mighty scourge of war will speedily pass away. Yet, if God wills that it continue, until all the wealth piled by the bond-man's two hundred and fifty years of unrequited toil shall be sunk, and until every drop of blood drawn with the lash shall be paid by another drawn with the sword, as was said three thousand years ago, so still it must be said 'the judgments of the Lord are true and righteous alltogether.' " Lincoln's faith is identical with that of the Hebraic prophets, who first conceived the idea of a meaningful history. If there was an element of scepticism in this grand conception, one can only observe that the Scripture itself, particularly in the book of Job, expressed some doubts about the exact definition in neat moral terms of the providential meanings of history. Incidentally, this eloquent passage surely expresses Lincoln's moral abhorrence of slavery. The point is important because the abolitionists expressed some doubt on this issue, since Lincoln was, as a responsible statesman, not primarily an abolitionist; but confessed "my primary purpose is to save the Union."

But the chief evidence of the purity and profundity of Lincoln's sense of providence lies in his ability, though the responsible leader of a great nation, embattled with secessionist States and naturally tempted to do what all political leaders, indeed all men, have done through the ages, to avoid the error of identifying providence with the cause to which the agent is committed. He resisted this temptation. Among all the statesmen of ancient and modern periods, Lincoln alone had a sense of historical meaning so high as to cast doubt on the intentions of both sides and to place the enemy into the same category of ambiquity as the nation to which his life was committed. Lincoln thus put the whole tragic drama of the Civil War in a religio-dramatic setting: "Neither party expected for the war, the magnitude, or the duration, which it has already attained. Neither anticipated that the *cause* of the conflict might cease with, or even before, the conflict itself should cease. Each looked for an easier triumph, and a result less fundamental and astounding. Both read the same Bible, and pray to the same God; and each invokes His aid against the other."

There follows an eloquent passage which puts the relation of our moral commitments in history to our religious reservations about the partiality of our moral judgments, more precisely than, I think, any statesman or theologian has put them. First the moral judgment, "It may seem strange that any men should dare to ask a just God's assistance in wringing their bread from the sweat of other men's faces." Then the religious reservation: "but let us judge not that we be not judged. The prayers of both could not be answered; that of neither has been answered just as they intended."

Surely this nice balance of moral commitment and religious reservation about the partiality of all historic commitments of biased men is a unique achievement and is particularly remarkable for a responsible political leader. For it is the very nature of political commitments that they make more ultimate claims for their cause, whether for the nation or their party, than either a transcendent providence or a neutral posterity would validate. Religious mystics and modern radical eschatologists have been neutral in specific disputes of history. But in that case they were morally uncommitted in a cause which was historically important. The ultimate consequence of this form of religious neutrality was to empty all historical striving of meaning and to invest the final end of history or an indifferentiated eternity with the fulfillment of human meaning at the price of reducing all historical striving to triviality.

It was Lincoln's achievement to embrace a paradox which lies at the center of the spirituality of all western culture; namely, the affirmation of a meaningful history and the religious reservation about the partiality and bias which the human actors and agents betray in the definition of meaning.

It was an important achievement to embrace this paradox. For the evil by-product of the historical dynamism of western culture was the fanaticism which confused partial meanings and contingent purposes with the ultimate meaning of life itself. The lack of fanaticism and the spirit of magnanimity in Lincoln were revealed in many of his policies, but most of all in his spirit toward the defeated secessionists, a spirit eloquently expressed in his Second Inaugural: "With malice toward none; with charity for all . . . let us strive on to finish the work we are in." Unfortunately, his untimely death at the hands of an assassin prevented him from carrying out his design of pacification and launched the nation into a terrible period of vindictive crushing of a vanquished foe, from which we have not yet recovered. The stubbornness of the South's resistance to the integration movement is part of the price we pay for the vindictiveness which Lincoln would have avoided.

But since the spirit of magnanimity was the fruit of his apprehension of the biased character of all historic judgments and did not annul those judgments, we must turn to Lincoln's scheme of moral principles, his hierarchy of values to ascertain the complexity of his compound of political and personal moral preferences. His abhorrence of slavery was variously expressed, but most eloquently in the previously quoted Second Inaugural. Yet he was not an abolitionist. He was quite frank in his letter to Horace Greeley in stating: "My primary purpose is to save the Union." This was the preference of a responsible statesman who felt himself sworn to "defend the Constitution." The secessionist, he said, "had no oath, registered in heaven," to destroy the Union. He himself had an oath to defend the Union. One might regard this preference as that of a patriot who expressed a nation's primal impulse of collective survival. But Lincoln's preference expressed not merely a national patriotism.

Lincoln had a Jeffersonian belief in the mission of the new nation to initiate, extend, and preserve democratic self-government. Thus not only national survival but the survival of democracy was involved in the fortunes of the Civil War.

In his brief and eloquent Gettysburg Address he defined the mission of the new nation in Jeffersonian terms: "Four score and seven years ago our fathers brought forth upon this continent, a new nation, conceived in Liberty, and dedicated to the proposition that all men are created equal. Now we are engaged in a great civil war, testing whether that nation, or any nation so conceived, and so dedicated, can long endure." Lincoln evidently believed that the whole democratic cause was being tested in the destiny of our own nation, a belief which was natural in the middle of the nineteenth century, when many European critics prophesied the failure of our system of government and when the trends of history which would make democracy a universal pattern of government in western Europe were not yet apparent. The peroration of the Gettysburg Address returned to the same theme: "That we here highly resolve that these dead shall not have died in vain — that this nation, under God, shall have a new birth of freedom — and that government of the people, by the people, for the people shall not perish from the earth."

Lincoln's passion for saving the Union was held by some critics to express a personal, and not necessarily a historical, concept of the irrevocable character of the covenant of the Constitution. A very high-minded leader of the secessionist states, Robert E. Lee, had a different conception. Though he abhorred slavery, he felt himself bound in loyalty to his State of Virginia, rather than to the nation. Since the Civil War itself, not to speak of the many unifying forces which made the nation one, subsequently altered the loyalties of our citizens, making state loyalty very subordinate to national loyalty, it is safe to say that, if Lincoln's conception of the irrevocable character of the national covenant was a personal conviction, it was also a conviction which his own contribution to the national destiny, and many forces even more far reaching than the Civil War, transmuted into a national conviction. In his First Inaugural he argued in favor of the irrevocable character of the covenant, in words which many of his contemporaries did not accept but which posterity now takes for granted. Said Lincoln: "I hold, that in contemplation of universal law, and of the Constitution, the Union of these states is perpetual. Perpetuity is implied, if not expressed, in the fundamental law of all national governments. It is safe to assert that no government proper, ever had a provision in its organic law for its own termination. To the extent of my ability I shall take care, as the Constitution itself expressly enjoins upon me, that the laws of the Union shall be faithfully executed in all the States."

Of course, there was a residue of moral ambiguity in his devotion to the national union. Sometimes his devotion included his abhorrence of slavery, for the Lincoln-Douglas debates were primarily on the question of allowing new states to decide the issue of slavery in each state. Lincoln, in opposing the policy, was a pure Jeffersonian. Thus he argued: "When he [Douglas] invites any people willing to have slavery, to establish it, he is blowing out the moral lights around us. When he says 'he cares not whether slavery is voted down or voted up,' that it is the sacred right of self government, he is in my judgment penetrating the human soul and eradicating the light of reason and the love of liberty in this American people."

This absolute rejection of slavery seems at variance

with the sentiment expressed in a letter to Horace Greeley, assuring him that his primary purpose is to save the Union and that, if he could save it half slave and half free, he would do it. The contradiction in the two attitudes may be explained by the fact that the point at issue in the Douglas debates was the extension of slavery into the free territories, as provided in the Kansas-Nebraska Act. Lincoln was violently opposed to this policy, the more so since he believed that if the institution were restricted to the original slave states, it would gradually die.

In this position he felt himself in firm accord with the founding fathers of the nation. He argued: "The framers of the Constitution found the institution of slavery among their other institutions at the time. They found that by an effort to eradicate it, they might lose much of what they had already gained. They were obliged to bow to the necessity. They gave power to Congress to abolish the slave trade at the end of twenty years. They also prohibited slavery in the territories where it did not yet exist. They did what they could and yielded to necessity for the rest. I also yield to all which follows from that necessity." (Speech at Springfield, July 17, 1858.)

In short, Lincoln's opposition to slavery cannot be questioned. If there is moral ambiguity in his position, it is an ambiguity which he shared with the founding fathers, indeed with the author of the Declaration of Independence, and, for that matter, with all responsible statesmen, who pursue their ideals within the frame of the harmony and survival of their community. In short, he exhibited not his own ambiguity, but the moral ambiguity of the political order itself.

Lincoln's attitude to the principle of the Declaration of Independence "that all men are created equal" was of course informed by the ethos of his day. It was not the same as the ethos of our own time, which is charged with eliminating the last vestiges of slavery from our national life. Lincoln's attitude on race equality exhibited the same fusion between the ideal of equality and the customary inequality which the institution of slavery had introduced into the ethos of the nation, which presumably characterized the attitude of Thomas Jefferson, the author of the Declaration.

In one of his debates with Senator Douglas, Lincoln said: "Last night Judge Douglas tormented himself with horrors about my disposition to make negroes perfectly equal with white men in social and political relations. I have said that I do not understand the Declaration to mean that all men are equal in all respects. They are not equal in color. But they are equal in their right to 'life, liberty and the pursuit of happiness'. Certainly the negro is not our equal in color, but still in the right to put into his mouth the bread his own hand earned, he is equal to every man, white or black." The affirmation of basic human equality is unexceptional. One might quarrel with the assumption that difference in color implies inequality. Lincoln either shared the color prejudices of his and our day, or he was political enough not to challenge popular prejudices too radically.

The chief source of tension between Lincoln and the abolitionists was Lincoln's hesitancy in freeing the slaves. That hesitancy was not personal, but motivated by a political calculation of a responsible statesman, namely, the loyalty of the border states. Lincoln reprimanded the commanders who freed the slaves in the border states, and when he issued the preliminary Emancipation Proclamation, postponed for a time until victory would insure that it was not regarded as a final desperate effort of a defeated nation, it was made applicable only to the Negroes in territories under Union arms. In the words of a distinguished historian, "It had the eloquence of a bill of lading."

Not only our own abolitionists, but the critical British liberals were not moved by the proclamation. But both its timing and its immediate scope were the fruits of statesmanlike calculations. They merely revealed that Lincoln was not a moral prophet in the first place, but a responsible statesman. All of his actions and attitudes can be explained and justified by his hierarchy of values, succinctly expressed in his statement to Horace Greeley, "My primary purpose is to save the Union."

A responsible statesman is compelled to relate all the moral aspirations and all the moral hesitancies of the social forces of a free society to the primary purpose of the survival of the community. In the political order justice takes an uneasy second place behind the first place of the value of internal order. In reviewing Lincoln's hierarchy of values, one must come to the conclusion that his sense of justice was strong enough to give that value an immediate position under the first purpose of national survival; and that the purpose of national survival included not only the physical life of the nation, but the system of democratic self-government, which he identified, perhaps too simply, as all our fathers did, with the survival of democracy throughout the world.

It may be significant that the moral ambiguities in the idealism of a responsible statesman proved themselves religiously superior to the pure moral idealism of the abolitionists, the Horace Greeleys, William Lloyd Garrisons, and Wendell Phillipses. This fact does not prove that responsible statesmen are morally superior to the pure idealists. In any case their idealist opposition to slavery was an indispensable contribution to the dramatic struggle which saved the nation and purged it of the hated institution of human bondage. In his message to Congress in 1862 Lincoln admirably revealed both the moral imperatives which prompted the emancipation and the political considerations which made him more cautious than the abolitionists approved.

The caution was prompted by diverse sentiments on the issue within the Union. Lincoln wrote: "Among the friends of the Union, there is great diversity, of sentiment, and of policy, in regard to slavery, and the African race amongst us. Some would perpetuate slavery; some would abolish it suddenly, and without compensation;

some would abolish it gradually, and with compensation; some would remove the freed people from us, and some would retain them with us, and there are yet other minor diversities. Because of these diversities, we waste much strength in struggles among ourselves. By mutual concession we should harmonize, and act together."

But Lincoln, as President, acted for the nation, and the moral imperative of the emancipation was eloquently expressed in the words: "In *giving* freedom to the *slave,* we *assure* freedom to the free — honorable alike in what we give, and what we preserve. We shall nobly save, or meanly lose, the last hope of earth. Other means may succeed; this could not fail. The way is plain, peaceful, generous, just — a way which, if followed, the world will forever applaud, and God must forever bless."

Lincoln's sense of the indivisibility of freedom and his conviction that the emancipation of the slaves implied the opportunity of "nobly saving the best hope of earth," the cause of democratic government, is particularly significant for a generation which is called upon to remove the last remnants of human bondage from our national life. It reminds us that as we give freedom we preserve our freedom and the prestige of free institutions. It is clear that Lincoln believed that in a nation, "conceived in liberty and dedicated to the proposition that all men are created equal," moral ambiguity is limited to the field of tactics and prompted by the diversity of opinion on the issue of slavery. But the ambiguity ends in the strategy. The emancipation of the slaves gives and preserves liberty, gives it to the slave and preserves it for all free men. The message to Congress throws light not on the moral problems of politics in general alone. It throws light on our own current political problems, especially that of integration.

But Lincoln's moral superiority over the idealists was not primarily due to his conscientiousness and power as a statesman. It was due to the depth and weight of his religious sense of the meaning of the drama of history, and his consequent sensitivity to the problem of the taint of self-interest in the definitions of meaning, by which human agents corrupt the meaning in which they are involved. It was due, finally, to the magnanimity which was the natural fruit of this sensitivity.

The idealists were, like most if not all idealists, self-righteous and consequently vindictive. Garrison may have made the southern response to the abolitionist movement more stubborn because he interpreted social attitudes and evils as if they were the fruits of criminal tendencies. He did not understand that good men may inherit social attitudes and become the bearers of social evil, although their own consciences are not perverse, but merely conventional.

This failure to understand the complex causes of historical and socially embedded evil helped generate the vindictiveness of the victors of the Civil War and the consequent horrors of Reconstruction days. As we try now, a century after the Civil War, to eliminate the last vestiges of slavery from our national life, we frequently encounter resentments in the South which are not so much the fruits of the terrible conflict as of the vindictiveness of Reconstruction; that is, of the harsh years when the North proved that, without humility, idealism can be easily transmuted into a cruel vindictiveness.

If we analyze the whole import of the relation of moral idealism to fanaticism, and of religious humility and contrition to magnanimity, and if we set the tension between Lincoln and the abolitionist in the context of this problem, the conclusion is inevitable that Abraham Lincoln is not only a statesman who saved the nation in the hour of its peril; he was also that rare and unique human being who could be responsible in executing historic tasks without equating his interpretation of the task with the divine wisdom.

It is, in short, not too much to claim that Lincoln embraced the paradox of all human spirituality, and of western historical dynamism in particular, more adequately than any statesman of modern history. The measure of his spiritual achievement will become fully apparent if we compare him with the religious, inspired idealists among the statesmen of the modern period from Oliver Cromwell to Woodrow Wilson.

On the
Gettysburg Address

by Robert Lowell

Abraham Lincoln was the last President of the United
States who could genuinely use words. He and Thomas
Jefferson are perhaps the only presidents with this gift.
Without his best speeches, Lincoln would have been less
great as a man of action; had he not been a great statesman, he could not have written his speeches. He knew
his occasion and sensed that whatever he said must have
the gravity and brevity of an act of state.

Last spring I was talking about the Gettysburg Address to a friend who is also a man of letters. He pointed
out to me its curious, insistent use of birth images:
"brought forth," "conceived," "created," and finally, a
"new birth of freedom."

Birth and Death!

The Gettysburg Address is a symbolic and sacramental act. Its verbal quality is resonance combined with a logical, matter of fact, prosaic brevity. It is part of the battle, a last military push that alters and adds significance to the previous military maneuvers. In his words, Lincoln symbolically died, just as the Union soldiers really died — and as he himself was soon really to die. By his words, he gave the field of battle a symbolic significance that it had lacked. For us and our country, he left Jefferson's ideals of freedom and equality joined to the Christian sacrificial act of death and rebirth. I believe this is a meaning that goes beyond sect or religion and beyond peace and war, and is now part of our lives as a challenge, obstacle, and hope. Lincoln's occasional speech of a hundred years ago still rings today when our country struggles with four almost insoluble spiritual problems: how to join equality to excellence, how to join liberty to justice, how to avoid destroying or being destroyed by nuclear power, and how to complete the emancipation of the slaves.

The Failure of Fredericksburg

UNDER THAT TRUE MAN AND SOLDIER,
MAJOR-GENERAL BURNSIDE

By Robert [T. S.] Lowell

Was nothing gained? Is this not gain, so high
    A mark for us and after-comers set?
Life is at strongest that can greatly die,
    And manhood better worth than all men get.

Is this not gain, that our slow, flabby heart,
    Dull-laboring, long, in sordid work and trade,
With quick, strong, throb thrown back to it should start,
    And learn that beat wherewith great deeds are made?

At need best blood may better far be shed
    Than frame fair thought, or drive the wheel and plough:
No fathers yet for country nobly bled,
    Whose sons are not the nobler livers now.

To push the bridge up to the flaming guns,
    To throng the rocking skiffs, in death's broad sight,
To wade the trench where their own life-blood runs, —
    This was to conquer, if they lost the fight.

They fail not, that their face still forward keep,
    And lift their stout hearts up from every fall:
They fail that in mid-stream dread greater deep;
    They fail, that, losing little, fear for all.

Here in far home, by safe ties tamely held,
   We shame to write of these things brave and high,
Though our own blood from its next veins has welled,
   And meekly we dare hope that we could die.

But shall your great deeds want their written fame;
   Our coward voices give you back no cheer?
To sit aghast or dumb were greater shame
   Than thus to warm to manhood, even here.

January 8, 1863

The above poem contained in *Poems by Robert Lowell,* published
in 1864, by E. P. Dutton & Co., Boston, p. 201.

Washington

By Robert Lowell

(Here published for the first time)

The heavy spokes of this wheel
touch the sore spots of the earth.

On the Potomac, swan-white
power launches keep breasting the sulphurous wave.

Otters slide and dive and slick back their hair.
Raccoons clean their meat in the creek.

In some hole of a museum, Commander Carpenter
still bombs the first German U-boat.

The circles are held by green statues, tough as weeds.
I cannot name the names, or number the dates,

or count the circles —
circle on circle, like rings on a tree.

They come here bright as dimes,
and die disheveled and soft.

May, 1964

The Significance
of Gettysburg

by Paul H. Douglas

I

Gettysburg has long exercised an emotional and intellectual fascination for all varieties of Americans. Both northerners and southerners have taken justified pride in the heroism of their soldiers and in their feats of arms. Students of military history and tactics have discussed the battle plans of the two commanders and the relative merits of Lee and Longstreet, Ewell and A. P. Hill on the one side, and of Meade and Hancock, Howard and Sickles on the other. Those with imagination have dwelt upon what may be termed the *mystique* of the battle and whether the result was indeed inevitable, or the consequence of shrewd moves and egregious blunders by the high commands, or whether it followed from the total responses of tens of thousands of individual men, many of whom, under great strain, responded heroically, while some sought safety in a less heroic manner. A few eminent writers such as Winston Churchill have attempted to speculate on what would have happened had the Confederates won the battle. Still others interested in the rhetoric as well as the fury of combat have centered their attention upon Lincoln's peerless words uttered four months later upon the dedication of the Union Cemetery and have compared them with Pericles' famous oration delivered twenty-three hundred years before or have traced his crucial final phrase to Theodore Parker through William H. Herndon. Finally, those primarily concerned with the long sweep of history have pondered over the effect which Gettysburg has had upon the life of our nation and the whole course of human freedom.

I realize that it is in a sense presumptuous for one who is not skilled in any of these arts to try his hand on a subject so much discussed. I realize also the overriding danger of polluting, in Periclean phrase, the memory of the heroic dead by inadequate comments. I also have a distinct aversion at seeing writing men with their pens and typewriters move front and center to take over the limelight from the fighting men whose deeds were written in blood, pain, and sacrifice. I start, therefore, with a distinct and justified sense of inadequacy.

Sometimes I have felt, in reading the accounts of our

battles in both the Civil War and in World War II, that the narrators had fallen into the reportorial fallacy of believing that because they were describing the course of events, they had somehow actually caused them to be. Let me say at once that I have no such illusions and that as one who, like millions of others, has walked over those once bloody but now peaceful slopes, my brief comments are written in reverence for the humble men in both armies who, for a complex of causes, struggled, were wounded, and died in this most bloody of battles for what they and the communities from whence they came believed to be both right and necessary.

II

But Gettysburg, like every critical human experience, invites analysis even today, for as Santayana once remarked, "those who cannot learn from history are doomed to repeat it." God deliver us from such a fate as that.

Tolstoi, in what I regard as the novel with the widest sweep ever written, *War and Peace,* uses the Napoleonic Wars, and in particular the invasion of Russia in 1812 and the battle of Borodino, to advance a theory of history which has found many supporters. For Tolstoi believed that it was the "inevitable march of events" which actually determined the destiny of peoples, and that individuals, whether of high or low station, were comparatively powerless to deflect, let alone to reverse, the stream of history. Tolstoi's military idol was Kutusov, who allowed events to happen instead of vainly seeking to impose a set plan upon them.

The modern follower of Tolstoi can, with good reason, apply this same theory to all that led up to Gettysburg, to the battle itself, and to its consequences. He could cite the determination of the southern slavocracy to carry slavery into the territories and possibly even into the free states, and the inevitable resistance which this aroused among the free farmers of the middle border and the idealists of the North. He could consider the election of Lincoln the inevitable result of the greater growth rate of the North and West and properly attribute the subsequent secession of the South to its failure to continue its control over the White House and Congress. He could describe the northern attempts to bring the war to an end by hastily trained masses of civilians as inevitably ending in successive defeats at Bull Run, on the Peninsula, at Fredericksburg, and at Chancellorsville. He could write that the failure of these efforts inevitably caused Lee to counterattack by moving north, and that the stiffened northern resistance created by fighting on home grounds led not only to the blunting of his attack at Antietam in 1862, but to its repulse in the hot July days at Gettysburg in 1863. The believers in inevitability have said that the greater manpower and superior economic resources of the North brought its inevitable triumph at Gettysburg. They have pointed out that the Confederacy was being slowly strangled in the West, that crucial backyard of the war which has been neglected by so many historians because neither the blunt middle westerners nor the slavocracy of the deep South have possessed the literary proclivities of the sons of Massachusetts and Virginia, who saw themselves at the center of every conflict and as the determining factor in every struggle.

There is indeed much to support the Tolstoyan theory in the battle of Gettysburg itself. Neither Lee nor Meade planned the battle. Instead the armies blundered into it. There is no evidence that Lee's celebrated attempt at double envelopment, which Rommel is supposed to have admired and copied, was consciously thought out. Once the northern forces had been driven eastward on the first day through the town of Gettysburg and had sought refuge on the high ground of Culp's Hill, it was simply common sense for Lee and Ewell to try to occupy those heights in order to cut the Union rear.

Similarly, when Dan Sickles recklessly left Little and Big Round Top unoccupied and moved out into an unduly advanced position in the peach orchard, it was merely standard procedure for Longstreet's men to attack and then to move on to the vacant hilltops. Nor did Meade really plan the disposition of the northern forces. He did not, in fact, arrive until the dawn of the second day and found his troops already on the heights of Culp's Hill and Cemetery Ridge and it was obvious that he should move some forces to his left. But even so, he did not fully recognize the importance of the two Round Tops and left them relatively unguarded. Nor was he fully prepared in advance to meet Pickett's immortal charge on the third day across the open mile between Seminary and Cemetery Ridges.

Another Tolstoi could therefore apply his doctrine of inevitability to Gettysburg to the repulse of Pickett and the retreat of Lee, and he could ascribe the failure of Meade to follow up and destroy the Confederate Army as due to the exhaustion of the northern armies, spiced with the possible desire of some of the Union generals not to win too sweeping a victory lest this result in the genuine emancipation of the Negroes.

But when one revisits Little Round Top and Culp's Hill on the Union left and right, respectively, and traces the military movements by the hours of the second day, it becomes very hard to hold to the doctrine of inevitability. For the sober truth is that the Confederates came within a hair's breadth of turning both Meade's left and right flanks, of penetrating his center, and of inflicting a crushing defeat upon the Union. The way to the Atlantic seaboard would then have been open. Harrisburg, Baltimore, and Philadelphia might quickly have fallen, and if the draft rioters could actually take over New York ten days *after* the victory at Gettysburg, what would they have done had Gettysburg been a northern defeat? Can we not see how Fernando Wood and possibly Horatio Seymour would have demanded peace on the basis of either the status quo ante or the recognition of the Confederacy? Let us remember also that the Copperhead movement was not only strong in the northern cities with its powerful organs such as the *New York World* and

The Chicago Times, but also in the southern sections of Ohio, Indiana, and Illinois. It will be remembered, moreover, that the mid-term elections of 1862 had, in the main, gone against Lincoln and the pro-war Republicans. Moreover, in England nearly all of the Establishment were partisans of the South and were anxiously waiting for some opportunity to press the cautious Palmerston Ministry into recognizing the Confederacy.

The turning of the Union flanks and the defeat of the Union army at Gettysburg, therefore, might well have meant the loss of the war with all the incalculable consequences which would have followed. It might well have meant the creation of two hostile nations in the middle of North America, one dedicated to slavery and the other to freedom. The former would have inevitably sought to create a slave empire so that as southern soil became exhausted, the slaves could then be taken to Mexico, to Central America, and to the sugar-rich islands of the Caribbean. North America would then have become another Europe with deadly wars periodically waged between the two contending nations. Athens and Sparta would have again been locked in internecine warfare, and Gettysburg would have been but a prelude to still greater struggles on a continent drenched with blood.

All these possibilities were inherent in the military situation on the late afternoon of July 2. It was not inevitable that they should fail to come to pass. For as the sun started to go down a spirited Confederate attack cut deeply into the northern center, while Culp's Hill on the Union right and Little Round Top on the left were on the point of falling into Confederate hands. Had this happened, it would have meant the loss of the battle, and probably of the war. To an Olympian observer of the battle in the waning hours of that day such an outcome must indeed have seemed inevitable.

That it failed to happen was not because of any grand strategy of the generals, but because the heroism of the Union troops and of the humble farmers, woodsmen, and city folks who comprised them interposed. The attack on the center was beaten off in a swirl of dust and blood. The regiments from New York, the Middle West, and New England, including the remnants of the famous Iron Brigade which had been forced to flee through the town of Gettysburg on the first day, rallied on the northern slopes of Culp's Hill. By furiously felling trees and digging trenches, they created bulwarks behind which they drove back wave after wave of attacks which at times came perilously close to the crest. Two citizen generals, Wadsworth and Greene, whose descendants and kinsmen have in our times graced Congress, held as firmly as their men. By the middle morning of the third day, Ewell's men had been beaten back and the Union right, although badly crippled and bent, was safe.

But an even greater disaster had nearly developed on the Union left. For through a series of incredible blunders, the commanding hills of the two Round Tops were left vacant and unoccupied save for a platoon of signalmen under G. K. Warren. After routing Sickles' corps in the peach orchard, regiments from Alabama and Texas actually took Big Round Top and were rushing up the slopes of Little Round Top through Devil's Den as the four regiments summoned by Warren ran to the top. A hand-to-hand conflict ensued in which the Top ran with blood. On the extreme left was the 20th Maine with its farmers, fishermen, and lumbermen commanded by Joshua L. Chamberlain, clergyman and former professor at my old college, Bowdoin. The Confederates were overpowering the Union defenses, and the capture of Little Round Top seemed imminent.

Had this happened, the Confederates would have brought their artillery to the top of the hill and on the next day would have forced Meade to withdraw — something which he was more than ready to do.

With their ammunition exhausted and the superior pressure of the Confederates about to take the hill, Chamberlain, the former professor of Greek, inspired perhaps by his memory of Herodotus' account of Miltiades' tactics at Marathon, ordered a bayonet charge. Just as surprisingly and with as much élan as the Greeks, it succeeded and Little Round Top was safe. And on the next day it was the Union artillery which was mounted on the hill and under Warren's direction tore bleeding gaps in Pickett's gray lines as they marched majestically to their doom.

There was therefore nothing inevitable in the final outcome, and Tolstoi's theory of history stands in need of serious modification.

The courage and resourcefulness of apparently humble men were the final determining factors. Even today, with all the terrible potentialities of nuclear and push-button warfare, these qualities are, in my judgment, finally decisive. The nations, statesmen, and military leaders who neglect these qualities do so at their peril. For men are not machines. They must feel that they have a just cause for which to contend and that the society in which they live respects not only them but their families, their friends, and their associates. As Sparta learned long ago, a helot class at home cannot be depended upon to defend their nation abroad. Free men fight best. But they must also know that others besides themselves are willing to sacrifice for the common good. A nation of self-seekers tends to fall apart. All this is as true today as it was at Marathon and Gettysburg. And freedom is more than a word to be uttered on the Fourth of July. It is not a semantic myth but a political, economic, and social reality upon whose presence, or absence, the fate of this nation may depend today as it did a century ago.

III

With Lee's defeat at Gettsyburg, the South's last chance to win the war was gone. A Union victory was not yet assured, and a draw was for a time possible. But despite profiteering at home and the blandishments of the Copperheads, the sorely tried farmers and workmen of the North held steady, and the sad-eyed son of the prairies refused to yield. It was then inevitable that the superior numbers and resources of the North would bring the final consequences of Gettysburg to fruition. Grant's sledge-hammer campaign of attrition in 1864 and 1865 involved terrible casualties to our forces, which an old Union surgeon, W. W. Keen, described to me sixty years afterward with horror. But while the absolute losses in Lee's army were somewhat less, their proportional loss was greater. This fact, together with the tightening grip of the Union armies in the West, and Sherman's tactics of total war as he marched from Atlanta to the sea and then up the coast, brought final military victory.

Gettysburg therefore ultimately meant that the political union forged between 1776 and 1787 would survive; that the Thirteenth Amendment would complete the Emancipation Proclamation; and that the Negroes would cease to be merely property like the cotton and sugar they produced, and would pass out from under chattel slavery. It meant, as Lincoln proclaimed on those same grounds, a little over four months later, that our nation, "conceived in liberty" and dedicated to the Jeffersonian doctrine which declared that all men were "created equal," would endure and would not perish from the earth. It meant that we would have at least the chance to develop a government which would not only be of the people, but by and for them as well. It meant that the dream of Jefferson, which Lincoln cherished in the very marrow of his bones, delineating a society where the rights of the people to life, liberty, and the pursuit of happiness were to be the primary concerns of government, had an increased chance of coming true. Something new in the long and bloody history of mankind might just possibly come into being on this continent if men and women would pursue these goals with half the ardor which the men who struggled in the stifling heat of those July days had displayed.

But it was the opportunity and not the certainty of realizing these ends that Gettysburg brought. For history is as indeterminate in peace as in war. It is one of the tragedies of the past century that in so many respects, despite great material progress, realization has fallen far short of the promise.

When peace came there was a surge of desire in the North to improve the position of the newly freed Negroes. It is a mistake to attribute this, as did my old teacher, William A. Dunning, and his host of southern disciples, to war-engendered hatred of the southern whites or to a desire to avenge the assassination of Lincoln and the attempted murder of Seward. These motives were no doubt real, but they were not all. For during those final years of the war, as is common at such times, in an effort to make the slaughter somehow seem worthwhile, the spirit of the Battle Hymn of the Republic had permeated the hearts of both the citizens and soldiers of the North. Idealism tempered and inspired by hope made men indeed willing to die to make men free. Ben Wade and Thad Stevens may well have been brutal and Charles Sumner unduly self-righteous. But with all their faults they wanted to help the Negro. Failing to give him land so that he could become economically independent, they sought however to provide him with education. Under General Oliver Otis Howard, who had lost his right arm at Fair Oaks, the Freedmen's Bureau, with help from the churches of the North, established schools and the primitive nuclei which have grown into the Negro universities of Howard, Fisk, and Atlanta. To protect the Negroes against the Black Codes, which had been passed by the white state governments set up by Lincoln and Johnson and which would have established qualified serfdom for the blacks, the congressional leaders were successful in getting the Fourteenth and Fifteenth Amendments enacted.

During the years from 1896 to 1935 when the Supreme Court mistakenly interpreted the due process clause in the Fourteenth Amendment as forbidding state action to protect the economically weak from the cumulative exactions of the strong, it was the fashion for many teachers of constitutional law to sneer at the amendment as the legal instrument by which the rising capitalist class had made itself immune from the just needs of the poor and from the judgments of the righteous.

There may have been a touch of truth in this. But the predominant purpose of the amendment was to make the Negro not a thing but a citizen; its aim was indeed to abolish all second-class citizenship and instead to make all men and women born or naturalized in the United States full-fledged citizens on equal terms with all others. They were, moreover, to be citizens of their nation as well as of their state and entitled to the equal protection of the laws with the same rights and privileges as all others. That this was also to be a national obligation was evidenced by the final section stating that Congress had the power by appropriate legislation to make the provisions of the Fourteenth Amendment actually effective. The same powers were subsequently placed behind the Fifteenth Amendment, which provided that the right of citizens to vote shall not be denied by the United States or any state on account of race, color, or previous condition of servitude. This in effect meant that no male over twenty-one should be deprived of the right to vote. Parenthetically, it may be remarked that once these rights were given to Negro males, it was inevitable that they would ultimately be accorded to women whether white or black. The wonder is that this took a full half-century to achieve. Then in 1873 and 1875, Congress passed the almost forgotten Civil Rights Statutes, or what may be termed as the Equal Public Accommodations Law of its time.

It has been the fashion ever since Dunning trained two full generations of southern historians to condemn the Reconstruction governments which were set up at this time in the southern states as incompetent and corrupt, with ignorant black masses directed by vicious carpet-baggers from the North such as Moses, Warmoth, and Ames. Here again there is an undoubted element of truth. But Raleigh, Columbia, Baton Rouge, and Jackson were little, if any, worse than Washington. For there

Sam Ward, the brother of the author of the Battle Hymn of the Republic and the king of the railway lobby, bought and sold congressmen and senators like cattle, while the saturnalia of corruption reached into the inner recesses of Grant's cabinet and his personal entourage. There were indeed few public figures in Washington who were left unsmirched.

But so strangely mixed are the qualities in any society, that the antislavery impulse, with a slower beat to be sure, lived on. Idealistic teachers continued to go South to do their bit in making the dream of Jefferson and Lincoln come true. And amid all the crudities and corruption of the southern capitals, genuine efforts were being made to establish a biracial democracy in which the former mudsills of the social order, regardless of color, were to be given the chance to raise themselves through education. But the election of 1876 put a stop to all this. The country, sickened by the corruption of the Grant Administration, really elected Tilden. But the Republicans, determined not to cede power, made a deal with certain representatives of the South that the electoral votes of South Carolina, Florida, and Louisiana would be switched to Hayes, and that he, in turn, would then withdraw the Union troops and allow the militant whites to take over.

Both sides lived up to their bargain. Tilden was duly counted out, and rather than provoke another civil war, the Democrats of the North acquiesced. Then the new southern governments began systematically to violate

the Fourteenth and Fifteenth Amendments and to reduce the Negroes to second-class citizenship. They cur-
tailed funds for Negro education. They gradually began
to pass sweeping segregation or Jim Crow ordinances.
Finally in the middle nineties, frightened by the growing
alliance of Negroes and whites in the Populist movement, they in effect deprived both groups of the right to
vote by means of poll taxes and other discriminatory
devices.

Rayford Logan is correct in terming the quarter-
century after 1877 the nadir of Negro rights. During this
period the humanitarian forces were spiritually in full
retreat. The Supreme Court in 1883 declared the Public
Accommodations Law of 1875 to be unconstitutional,
and thirteen years later in the celebrated case of *Plessy* v.
Ferguson held a Louisiana statute prescribing segregation to be constitutional. The purposes of the Fourteenth
and Fifteenth Amendments were being forgotten, forgotten, that is, by all in high station save one noble jurist,
John Marshall Harlan of Kentucky, himself a former
slaveowner but a Union soldier who understood and passionately believed in human freedom. This last of the
Romans dissented in both of these cases in opinions
which I prophesy will be forever cherished in the annals
of American freedom. He alone had the bravery to pro-
claim that the Constitution was "color blind." But
despite Harlan, all but one of the Civil Rights Statutes
were either repealed or nullified. Lynchings became
frequent. Prejudice against the Negroes began once

again to permeate the North, so that spiritually the victory at Gettysburg began to ebb away. And in 1909 in Lincoln's home town of Springfield, a Negro was actually lynched, and because of that shame a handful of conscience-smitten men and women founded the National Association for the Advancement of Colored People.

Indeed, during the sixty years which followed 1877, the people of the North became not only more and more tired of their former concern but somewhat ashamed of it. Historians began systematically to denigrate the great antislavery leaders such as William Lloyd Garrison and Wendell Phillips, to sprinkle rose water over slavery, and to make Reconstruction, not slavery, the great crime of the nineteenth century. Well might the ghost of Bob Toombs have exulted from the foot of Bunker Hill Monument over the spiritual triumph of his ideas.

Only in recent years has there come a spiritual revival amongst both blacks and whites. As the Negroes moved into the cities, both North and South, they became somewhat more independent and less servile than they had been as field hands upon the plantations or as tenant farmers. Where a two-party system existed, the parties sought their support and in return had to give something. The level of education among the Negroes rose steadily. As the industrial unions won recognition in the great mass production industries of steel, automobiles, rubber, and all varieties of machinery as well as in clothing, they admitted Negroes to full membership and gave them both enhanced status and training in self-government. As the races of Africa stirred, won independence, and shook off British, French, and Belgian control, the pride of the Negroes in their African origins and heritage rose, and they began to ask themselves why they could not realize in this country the promise of the two great postwar amendments.

The struggle for the effective right to vote and for the elimination of segregation in education was waged primarily by the N.A.A.C.P. with some aid from the industrial unions and the rising numbers of the morally concerned. Finally the Supreme Court in two epoch-making decisions unanimously reversed *Plessy* v. *Ferguson* and declared segregation in the public schools to be a violation of the Fourteenth Amendment.

But except in the border states actual progress in this direction has been disappointingly slow. Similarly, the much vaunted electoral laws of 1957 and 1960 have proved, as some of us prophesied at the time, to be relatively ineffective. During these last few years, in protest against the glacial rate of progress, Negro and white youths and concerned ministers, both white and black, have taken to direct action of a Ghandian type. In the minds of most Negroes, there is undoubtedly an inevitable and justifiable resentment against the whites for the three hundred years of bitter wrongs which they have suffered since they were brought by force to this continent. Their racial memories still burn with searing thoughts of the horrors of the slave ships, the humiliation of the auction block, the brutality of the commercial slave system under the lords of the lash, the denial of family life, and the social humiliations they have experienced during the century since emancipation. It is a sad but undeniable fact that we cannot erase history. For what the moving finger of time has written stays on in the memory coils of the race and neither our "piety nor wit shall lure it back to cancel half a line nor all [our] tears wash out a word of it."

But in the main, up to now, the Negro movement has conquered man's natural tendency to return evil for evil and has practiced instead not only nonviolent resistance but spiritual superresistance. Under the noble leadership of such members of their race as Philip Randolph, Roy Wilkins, Martin Luther King, and Ralph Abernethy, they have borne their sufferings not only with dignity but with much all encompassing love toward their oppressors. What could have been more impressive than the great outpouring in Washington on the 28th of last August, when a quarter of a million Americans marched with beating hearts and steady step to the Lincoln Memorial and there addressed their appeals to the conscience of the nation? To those who took part and to the multitudes who watched and listened, it was the moving experience of a lifetime.

These practical applications of the teachings of Jesus have struck surprise and anger into the hearts of many whites. To see a despised race demonstrate spiritual superiority has been a blow to the self-esteem of many which they have found impossible to bear and which has provoked them to greater fury.

In thinking over the significance of this last century, let us note that the emancipation of the Negroes was forced by blood upon the South, and that it came from Gettysburg and its sister battles and not from any wholesale conversion of the heart. Because the country had refused to follow the way of John Woolman, who by persuasion and entreaty got his fellow Quakers of the eighteenth century to free their slaves without compensation, we were compelled to take the way of John Brown with Grant and Sherman to boot. Since it was an unwilling and a forced emancipation, we in this country have not made as smooth and humane a transition from slavery to freedom as have Brazil or the British islands of the Caribbean.

Let the skeptic who doubts whether the issues are real read only the heaped up studies of the President's Commission on Civil Rights to see the terrible handicaps and humiliations under which Negroes suffer because of their color, as voters, in the schools, before the courts, in employment, and in the countless indignities of daily life. Few would have the courage of the intrepid Texan who recently had himself colored black in order to taste these experiences at first hand. But can we not imaginatively re-create them by asking ourselves how we would feel if, because of the accident of birth, we were compelled to suffer daily as they?

And without wishing to take an unfair advantage of

those who think and feel differently, may we all ponder the significance of Jesus' saying "Inasmuch as ye have done it unto one of the least of these my children, ye have done it unto me also."

IV

We now find ourselves to be in almost as crucial a position as during the 1850's and with many striking similarities with that decade.

Now, as then, we face a great moral issue. Now, as then, there are large numbers working and praying for reform. These are men and women who have all the imperfections which loom so large to critical contemporaries and are so little forgiven by them, but who have nevertheless a desire to retrieve the dark mistakes of the past. In scriptural terms, they hunger and thirst after righteousness not merely for themselves but also for the society in which we live and for our beloved country.

Now, as then, imminent matters of public policy face the Congress with men in both parties striving for much the same goals as did Chase and Sumner.

Now, as then, there is stubborn opposition from men whose private characters are highly estimable and whose social bearing is commonly far more pleasing than that of the advocates of civil rights. And to complete the analogy, many discerning students fancy that they see a striking resemblance between the conduct of the parties and the structure of the Congress now with what it was then. In my party they fancy that they see not only the

Jefferson Davises and the Robert Toombses, but also the Jesse Brights, the Franklin Pierces, and the James Buchanans. They claim also to see the modern reincarnations of Stephen A. Douglas of Illinois, whose seat I now occupy, refusing to take a stand on the moral issues of the day and seeking a surface harmony which basically does not exist.

And in the party of Lincoln across the aisle, these same observers allege that there sit once again the flesh and blood embodiments of Zachary Taylor, Millard Fillmore, Henry Clay, and Daniel Webster. For these were men who, by refusing to take a stand, led a great historic party down the road to deserved oblivion and who, because they blew neither hot nor cold, were finally spewed from the mouth of God and whose shades like those whom Dante saw at the gates of the Inferno dwell forever in that gray twilight which knows neither victory nor defeat.

Perhaps these analogies are fanciful; perhaps they are false. I hope they are. But the coming months will tell.[1]

If Gettysburg tells us anything, it is that nothing is inevitable. The opponents of civil rights are strongly entrenched. They occupy the heights of legislative power. They possess most of the crucial chairmanships and largely control the strategic committees. They are skilled parliamentarians and men of personal charm as were

[1] This was written in January, 1964. Happily both parties rose to the occasion and these well-grounded fears did not come true. After a long struggle Congress passed a good civil rights law in July.

Jefferson Davis and Alexander Stephens. And in the Senate they possess the mighty weapon of the filibuster, which has been described by a widely read southern columnist as "the South's never ending revenge for Gettysburg." With all this and with the help of their many secret sympathizers, they believe that they can wear out the forces of civil rights and either cause them to tire and quit the battle, as they did in the '70's, or provoke the youthful and impatient to violence and thus discredit them, or force such an emasculation of the final bill as to rob it, as in 1957 and 1960, of meaningful significance.

This may indeed happen. If it does, I am afraid that the Roy Wilkinses and Martin Luther Kings will be pushed aside by the mass of Negro youths who will turn to more violent leaders and methods with an incalculable loss to themselves and to our country. For violence in the very nature of the case is commonly met with violence and hate engenders hate.

As a white man, I do not feel justified in offering advice to the Negro race about what they should do. But it is proper, I believe, to point out what their worst enemies would have them do. And again, without forcing the analogy, I believe that we face in the winter of 1964 something of what the nation faced in the summer of 1863.

May I therefore urge my associates in the ranks of the civil rights army to observe the same energetic steadfastness in the cause of freedom which the men of the Union displayed on Culp's Hill, Little Round Top, and at the clump of trees in the center of the Union lines where the final agonized gasp of the battle was uttered?

May I also urge that we wage our battle without the slightest touch of personal or sectional self-righteousness? Our cause is indeed righteous but we ourselves have often lived and strayed away from the paths of righteousness. We recognize that in our personal lives and in our communities we have often been guilty of prejudice and of other grave faults and have failed to live by our faith. For all this, we ask forgiveness and pray that by our conduct we may now redeem ourselves from these grave blots.

Nor should we claim too much for our sections. The North was spared the curse of slavery not by any superior virtue but by the fortunate accident of climate and geography. But northerners were the most cruel masters of the slave ships, and Harriet Beecher Stowe properly made the brutal overseer, Simon Legree, a Yankee. Even today we of the North and West often lack the warmth of human fellowship with all the under-privileged which is the characteristic of the gentler elements of the South.

I urge therefore that as we wage our struggle with determination, that we do so without hatred and with a full appreciation of the personal virtues of those who oppose us.

As Hancock, the superb and dauntless general, waited calmly but with beating heart on the western slopes of

Cemetery Ridge to repulse the heroic charge of Pickett's men, he spied two old friends and comrades, Lewis Armistead and Dick Garnett, leading their dauntless troops across the valley of death. Hancock directed the effective resistance which won the final battle, but he paid honor to his antagonists in the bittersweet relationship of old friends locked in battle. May not we profit from his noble yet gentle example?

Unknown
at This Address

by David C. Mearns

It is with unsuppressed embarrassment and grave mis-
giving that I realize how audacious, futile, and, perhaps,
unkind is my self-imposed assignment. Let it, then, be
forlornly and shamefully blurted out that it is not my
object to *add* one mite, whit, tittle, iota, jot, or what-
you-will to the abundant stores of Lincoln learning, but,
conversely and deliberately, to subtract from them. My
purpose, in other words, is not to diffuse enlightenment,
but to stagger in darkness; not to diminish, in any sense,
his own gigantic stature, but, rather, only to reduce,
however slightly, our own credulity, our own unreasoned
acceptance of whatever we are told, and to display the
savage voracity of our own Lincoln-whetted appetites.

The question may well be asked: why select a topic so impolite, disturbing and destructive of the inanities of innocence? By way of answer, let it be said that those who have closely watched, followed, examined, and have lived long with the Lincoln story have reached the inevitable and uncomfortable conclusion that we know entirely too much about the venerable gentleman. This is especially true when our so-called "knowledge" is (as it is too often) mistaken, unfounded, distorted, perjured, easily contradicted, or, simply, untested by the most elementary rules of evidence. We have, I am ready to believe, reached a point where we must begin to *unknow* Lincoln. Our own sanity requires it; common courtesy to his memory sternly compels it.

As long ago as the end of the last century, Max Beerbohm defined the situation, when he wrote: "History does not repeat itself. The historians repeat one another." Certainly, this baneful tendency has grotesquely mutilated the Lincoln story, but there have been other factors comparably and appallingly insidious. Foremost among these perverting influences has been the treatment applied to Mr. Lincoln by his ancient associates and companions. Ordinarily men of probity and honor, their personalities were mysteriously altered whenever they clutched those air-borne coattails.

Almost without exception, these worthies developed two common characteristics: they grossly exaggerated the intensity of their intimacy with the late Mr. Lincoln, and they postponed the writing of their recollections until they had grown dim and tarnished, or had vanished altogether. This last deficiency they supplied by releasing all of their gifts of fancy, describing, in infinite detail and with rich specificity, episodes and conversations which had never taken place. One of these old cronies even went so far as to purchase his reminiscences from another and then retained a ghost to put them in shape for publication. Thus it seems likely that the shade of Mr. Lincoln must have spent the early years of immortality sadly repeating John Clare's lines composed in the Northampton County Asylum:

> I am! yet what I am who cares, or knows?
> My friends forsake me like a memory lost.

Certainly *his* friends and acquaintances had been quick to lose their memories, and their inventive productions should be consigned to the appendices to Gayley's *Ancient Myths* and Bulfinch's *Age of Fable,* where they cannot be confused with admissible historical testimony.

We, the public, have been the sufferers from this alliance of those historians, who lack an urge to enquiry, with those Lincoln contemporaries, whose imaginations were distended to the point of explosion. Together they are like the Bellman's pronouncement in *The Hunting of the Snark:* "I have said it thrice: What I tell you three times is true."

This, it seems to me, is reason enough to set about at once to unknow Lincoln. Let us, then, take as a clinical study the baffling case of the Gettysburg Address which has so recently celebrated its centennial. What do we know about it? What have we been told about it? Come, spread it on the dissecting table. Ask the questions. Find, if you can, the answers.

As a random beginning, did Mr. Lincoln receive a *printed* invitation to attend the dedicatory ceremonies at the soldiers' cemetery, in Gettysburg, on Thursday, November 19, 1863? It has been said over and over again, and as recently as in an article published in *Life* for November 15, 1963, that he did. Now it is not impossible, it is not even improbable, that some printed invitations were issued, although I have never seen one. What may be said with more assurance is that there is no record to support the supposition that one was sent to Mr. Lincoln.

It was, of course, David Wills, in his capacity as the agent of the Governor of Pennsylvania, who wrote to Mr. Lincoln on November 2, asking him to participate in the exercises, and formally to "set apart these grounds to their sacred use."

How and when did Mr. Lincoln acknowledge the request? Did he, as would have been natural, write directly to Mr. Wills, or did he, by messenger and word of mouth, transmit his acceptance, or, which would have been surprising in one as meticulous in such matters as was he, did he not respond at all? These are the alternatives, but there is no documentation to fix the choice. All that is known is that, within a week, the public press reported that "President Lincoln has determined to be present at the consecration."

121

By whatever medium his consent was transmitted, its tentative and provisional tone may be reconstructed from a letter which Mr. Wills wrote to William H. Seward, Secretary of State, on November 14: "His Excellency, the President . . . will be present at the consecration . . . unless prevented by unforeseen circumstances, and will, with some remarks, formally dedicate . . . the grounds where the burials are being made. In the event of his not being able to be present that duty would, I think, naturally devolve on you."

When did Mr. Lincoln commence the preparation of his speech? It is impossible to establish the date. Noah Brooks, a house painter turned journalist, generally considered a reliable source, told in articles published in *Scribner's Monthly* for February, 1878, and in *The Century Magazine* for January, 1895, how, on Sunday, November 15, 1863, he had accompanied Mr. Lincoln to Alexander Gardner's photographic studio, on Washington's Seventh Street, and how he had carried with him an advance copy of Edward Everett's oration, which had been printed in the shop of the *Boston Journal*. According to Brooks it occupied "nearly the whole of two pages . . . and looked very formidable indeed." Brooks asked the President if he had composed his own text. "Well, no," was the reply. "It is not exactly written. It is not finished anyway. I have written it over two or three times, and I shall have to give it another lick before I am satisfied. But it is short, short, short."

This Brooks account is deeply imbedded in Lincoln

literature. It has been quoted, paraphrased, and cited hundreds, perhaps thousands, of times. Through constant repetition it has gained an aura of sanctified authenticity. It turned up, without challenge to its credibility, in an introduction, written not so long ago by a distinguished Harvard professor, for a publication of our oldest historical society.

But Brooks was mistaken; his faithful adherents have been misled. By way of proof, witness the entry in Edward Everett's diary for Saturday, November 14: "Sent the manuscript of the address to the office of the Daily Advertiser, in which it fills 6-¼ columns & received back proof sheets of the whole by 5 o'clock in the afternoon, as well & correctly set up, and the proofs after my correction as clean as any that ever passed through my hands."

This, to use an ancient phrase, puts the kibosh on the Brooks fantasy.

It was not the press of the *Boston Journal,* as Brooks averred, but, rather, the press of the *Daily Advertiser* to which the manuscript was sent. It did not fill "nearly the whole of two pages," as Brooks claimed, but, on the contrary, only six and a quarter columns. Finally, there is a third and completely devastating rebuttal: it would have been utterly impossible for Mr. Lincoln to receive one of the advance copies as promptly as the following day. It is this last consideration which lends a touch of charming irrelevance to the decision of the learned joint authors of *Lincoln in Photographs,* made in an effort to reconcile irreconcilables, that the dialogue actually took place as early as November 8.

Did Mr. Lincoln read aloud his address before his departure for Gettysburg? Ward Hill Lamon, the President's former law partner, who was then Marshal of the District of Columbia, used to give this account:

> A day or two before the dedication, Mr. Lincoln told me he would be expected to make a speech on the occasion; that he was extremely busy, with no time for preparation, and that he greatly feared he would not be able to acquit himself with credit, much less to fill the measure of public expectation. From his hat (the usual receptacle of his private notes and memoranda) he drew a page of foolscap, closely written, which he read to me, first remarking that it was a memorandum of what he intended to say.

This reminiscence, with variations and omissions, was published at least three times: in the Philadelphia *Times* for October 4, 1887 (twenty-four years after the event), then in *The Washington Critic* for February, 1888, and later, between hard covers, in his *Recollections of Abraham Lincoln,* as edited by his daughter, Dorothy Lamon Teillard, and issued in 1911. In the earlier versions he insisted that what he heard "a day or two before the dedication" was, as he put it, "in substance, and I think, *in haec verba,* what was printed as his Gettysburg speech. " As time went on, however, Lamon seems to have lost confidence in the indelibility of his memory, for in its final rendering, he qualified the phrase to read, "in substance, if not in exact words." This is enough, it seems to me, to cast dubiety on his subsequent assertion, otherwise unsupported and probably apocryphal, that Lincoln regarded his address, as delivered, a flat and flagrant failure. Yet despite its implicit trumpery, the Lamon legend has become a hardy perennial that seeds itself far and wide. It is time to do some weeding in the Lincoln literature.

Did Mr. Lincoln write any part of his address on the train from Washington to Gettysburg? The belief that he did gained its broadest and deepest currency as a result of Mary Raymond Shipman Andrews' *The Perfect Tribute,* published in 1906. Mrs. Andrews, it is said, got the story from her son, Paul Shipman Andrews, who got it from Walter Burlingame, who got it from Anson Burlingame, who got it from Edward Everett. It descended, in other words, from mouth to mouth, and, must have been embellished and enhanced along the way. A correspondent of mine has written:

I wish I could help you on *The Perfect Tribute* mystery but I'm afraid I can't. The story seems to have passed through so many hands, including those of my imaginative Uncle Walter that I am afraid historical inaccuracies were inevitable.

For my own part, I have read most of Mrs. Andrews's extremely saccharine fiction . . . and it has never occurred to me to take any of it seriously as authentic history. She was a darling person and it is a pity she insisted on writing.

The notion that Mr. Lincoln had prepared the address, while on his way to Gettysburg, had been categorically rejected twelve years before by John George

Nicolay, who, in the February, 1894, issue of *The Century* had written:

There is neither record, evidence, nor well-founded tradition that Mr. Lincoln did any writing, or made any notes, on the journey between Washington and Gettysburg. The train consisted of four passenger coaches, and either composition or writing would have been extremely troublesome amid all the movement, the noise, the conversation, the greetings, and the questionings which ordinary courtesy required him to undergo in these surroundings; but still worse would have been the rockings and joltings of the train, rendering writing virtually impossible.

This disclaimer, coming, as it did, from so eminent a source, should have delivered the coup de grace to shadowy hearsay. As Primate, Mr. Nicolay stood at the high altar of orthodox Lincolnology. He had been the President's private secretary and had accompanied him to Gettysburg; he was custodian of the Lincoln papers; he was (with Colonel Hay) Mr. Lincoln's authorized biographer and editor. These privileges and attainments made his article definitive and placed it beyond the reach of disparagement and derogation. Since its publication, it has become the rock upon which the proliferate literature has been built.

For this reason, I must stand accused of impiety and irreverence when I say, as I say now, that it is so filled with error, inaccuracy, and omission as to make one wonder in what particulars it may be regarded as holy writ. It is, on the other hand, easy to condone Mr. Nicolay's consistent confusion. His subject was already thirty-one years old; time had wrought its erosions. His eyes were troubling him. He was confronted with an intolerable deadline, which commanded haste.

It should be added, in all fairness, however, that there were those who supported Mr. Nicolay's position. One of them was James Barnet Fry, Provost Marshal-General, who had been Mr. Lincoln's military escort on the trip, and who, as early as 1886, wrote: "It has been said, I believe, that Lincoln wrote in the car *en route* to Gettysburg the celebrated speech which he delivered upon that historic battle-ground. I am quite sure that is an error. I have no recollection of seeing him writing or even reading his speech during the journey. In fact, there was hardly any opportunity for him to read or write."

An odd twist was given in an interview, published in the New York *Sun,* for April 3, 1887; these are the pertinent passages:

"I saw one of the most splendid compositions in the English tongue written," said ex-Congressman Edward McPherson, while chatting about some of his recollections of Lincoln recently. "I believe that it is admitted now by scholars that for sublimity of thought, simplicity and yet elegance of expression, lucidity and purity of diction, Mr. Lincoln's brief oration at the dedication of the National Cemetery at Gettysburg takes place with the loftiest specimens of oratory. . . . Yet Mr. Lincoln wrote it on his knee in a railroad car. It was practically an extemporaneous composition; that is, in the sense that it was wholly unpremeditated. He simply committed to paper the thought that was uppermost in his mind, and he had no idea whatever that he had written anything more than a passing thought in the event that he was to assist in commemorating.

"I represented the Gettysburg district in Congress at the time of the battle, and at the dedication of the cemetery Mr. Lincoln was my guest. He was not sure that he could be present when he was first asked, but said that he should go to Gettysburg if possible. I think he was not prepared to say positively that he would go until a very few hours before the time set for leaving Washington. So he could not have given any thought to the oration before. I was his seat mate in the car, and though he talked pleasantly, and spoke of the country through which we were passing, yet I thought he was laboring with one of those spells of profound melancholy with which he was at times afflicted. He spoke of Mr. Everett, who was to deliver the chief oration, and said that Everett ought to be at his very best. I knew that Mr. Everett had given even more than his usual care in preparing his oration, and looked upon his work as a masterpiece, and I believe I told Mr. Lincoln so, and he said that the theme was great enough to inspire such an orator as Everett to his best. Mr. Lincoln, I think, had not thought of saying anything himself, but I told him that he would be expected to make a few remarks, for it would not be permitted him to be silent. He sat for some moments absorbed in thought, and at last began to feel in his pockets, as if for loose paper. I asked him if he wanted paper and pencil, and he said 'Yes, a scrap of paper,' and I opened my valise and gave him two or three sheets of note paper. He drew up his long knees, and, putting a book on them, wrote, jotting down, as I supposed, a few heads or suggestions. He wrote right along, without hesitation or erasure, and filled one page and a part of another. Then he folded it up and put it in his pocket, simply saying that he had set down a few lines that had occurred to him to say."

128

This discursive verbiage is bewildering. It is even more bewildering to read the letter which McPherson wrote to Horatio King some ten months later: "I never said to anyone, anywhere, one word of what was attributed to me by a N. Y. Sun correspondent about a year ago. I at once contradicted it by letter & through the Associated Press but I do not know to what extent the denial was printed. The 'interview' turns up every now & then. . . . I did not ride with Lincoln to Gettysburg or elsewhere, & the whole statement is a falsification."

Ponder now the curious aberration of Major-General Julius A. Stahel, who, in 1911, wrote: "I escorted President Lincoln from Washington to Gettysburg, and was with him in the same car when he wrote something on his knee, which I fully believe was the famous address which he delivered on the battlefield." But General Stahel was not on the same train. He was, at this time, in command of a division in the Department of the Susquehanna stationed in Harrisburg. He came to Gettysburg on the Governors' Special which did not reach its destination until five hours after Mr. Lincoln's arrival.

Andrew Carnegie must not be overlooked. He is reported to have told Herbert Spencer and Charles M. Schwab, on different occasions, how he, when secretary to Thomas A. Scott, president of the Pennsylvania Railroad, had accompanied Lincoln to the scene of the address, and how, in the course of the journey, Lincoln had borrowed his pencil to do some writing. Plausibility is lent to the tale by those who have transcribed a note, dated November 17, written by Edwin M. Stanton, Secretary of War, to Mr. Lincoln, in these words: "The arrangement I proposed has been made. The train will leave the Depot at 12 o'clock. I will assign the Adjutant General or Colonel Fry to accompany you, and to control the train. A. Carnegie will call for you at 12." Stanton's calligraphy was, to be sure, extremely difficult to decipher, but it is certain that what he wrote was not "A. Carnegie," but, rather, "A carriage." Mr. Carnegie was not in Washington on November 18.

Despite hoaxes and the spurious, and whether or not well-founded, the tradition did exist. It existed as early as the earliest biographers. Isaac Newton Arnold, for example, in his *History of Abraham Lincoln,* published in Chicago in 1866, wrote: "President Lincoln, while on his way from the Capitol to the battle-field, was notified that he would be expected to make some remarks. Retiring a short time he prepared the . . . address." Josiah Gilbert Holland, in *The Life of Abraham Lincoln,* published at Springfield, Massachusetts, in 1866, asked and answered the rhetorical question: "Did Mr. Everett say more or better in all his pages than Mr. Lincoln said in these lines? Yet they were written after he left Washington and during a brief interval of leisure." Harriet Beecher Stowe, in *Men of Our Times,* published at Hartford, in 1868, made this comment: "Perhaps in no language, ancient or modern, are any number of words found more touching and eloquent than his speech of November 19, 1863. . . . He wrote it in a few moments, while on the way to the celebration." As late as 1885, the President's son, Robert Todd Lincoln, would declare: "My father's Gettysburg Address was jotted down in pencil, in part at least, on his way to the place."

Weigh now, if you will, the evidence given by Mr. Lincoln's fellow travelers. The first to testify was John P. Usher, who, as Lincoln's Secretary of the Interior, had been aboard the train. In 1882, Mr. Usher, then Mayor of Lawrence, Kansas, deposed that "on the cars, between the national capital and Gettysburg, upon a piece of cardboard placed upon his knee, with a great crowd all around him, talking, gossiping, laughing and chattering, he wrote the words."

Henry Clay Cochrane, then a second lieutenant in the Marine Corps, was ordered to accompany the Marine Band to Gettysburg. This afforded him an opportunity closely to watch the President. Writing in 1907, Cochrane recalled:

At Baltimore, General Schenck, who then commanded that district, and his staff, joined us, and soon after the President went forward in the car and seated himself with a party of choice spirits, among whom was Mayor Frederick W. Lincoln of Boston. They told stories for an hour or so, Mr. Lincoln taking his turn and enjoying it very much. Then, when approaching Hanover Junction, he arose and said: "Gentlemen, this is all very pleasant, but the people will expect me to say something to them to-morrow, and I

131

must give the matter some thought." He then returned to the rear room of the car. . . . My . . . belief is that the first nineteen lines were written in Washington and the remainder on the train and in Gettysburg.

Summon now to the stand James Wall Scully, native of Ireland, who had risen in the ranks from private to lieutenant-colonel. Scully was on a twenty-day leave of absence, recovering from injuries suffered by being run over by a handcar, when he was temporarily attached to General Schenck's staff and joined the Presidential entourage, at Baltimore. In 1909 Scully waxed emphatic, insisting:

I was introduced to the President, and rode in his car to Gettysburg.

Now, it has been said and written, over and over again, that Mr. Lincoln did not write that address while on the way; and in fact prominent persons have denied that he wrote it at all; but while a hundred or more, may not have seen him write it, their testimony is altogether negative, but I know that at least half a dozen *did see him* write it, and of whom *I was one.* I saw him take a pad from the hand of some one; sit down in his "state room;" and write *something that he held in his hand while delivering that speech.*

Similar statements have come down to us from such respectable contemporaries as Benjamin Perley Poore, correspondent of the *Boston Daily Journal* and Congressman James M. Ashley, of Ohio. If, as all the circumstances indicate, Mr. Lincoln left Washington dissatisfied with the concluding lines of his script, it would be surprising if he did not brood on them as the wheels turned, and jot down a revisionary phrase or